ZIMBABWE'S HEAVENLY RUINS

Zimbabwe's Heavenly Ruins

A mystery explained

Richard Ganter

UPFRONT PUBLISHING
LEICESTERSHIRE

Zimbabwe's Heavenly Ruins

ISBN 1-84426-111-5

First published 2003 by
UPFRONT PUBLISHING LTD
Leicestershire

Typeset in Bembo by
Bookcraft Ltd, Stroud, Gloucestershire
Printed by Lightning Source

CONTENTS

ACKNOWLEDGEMENTS

My heartfelt thanks to my parents, and for their constant encouragement and love: without them this book would not have been possible. Thank you too to Brigitte and Christa who shared the early travels in Africa, and to Rosanna Rodriguez and C.R.J. 'Niels' van Rooyen's African vibes.

ILLUSTRATIONS

I

UNDER AFRICAN SKIES

> 'Dawning as a falcon', he reaches the celestial realm of Ra on the 'Imperishable Star' and is placed on the throne of Osiris ...
>
> *Pyramid Text of King Pepi:*
> *The Pharaoh's Journey to the Afterlife*

Under African skies the air is clear, and the stars on the horizon seem as close to touch as the smell of the African bush.

This is March 1985, a clear crisp night. The tent is pitched right outside the entrance of the Great Zimbabwe ruins. Complete stillness in the darkness of an African night. In the remote distance a soft sound of drums beating.

For many hours I lie on my back gazing at the stars overhead – a magnificent sight that can only rarely be observed in our industrialised polluted age: all the more important to cherish these moments when you are one with the earth and in touch with the universe.

The reasons for coming here were twofold: first a journey that would eventually take me 4000 miles overland through Africa, and second a return to the only place in sub-Saharan Africa that boasts these unusual man-made stone structures from an unknown civilisation. Many questions about their origins remain unanswered. Why build such a magnificent piece of structure without mortar? And why in this location in southern Africa?

In 1969, in my early childhood, my first visit to these ruins left a very deep mark on the memories of early travel. That visit was during the hottest summer months at New Year, when the average temperature would reach 35°C. This time I arrived in autumn, when the green hills of south-eastern Zimbabwe give rise to calmness and serene beauty.

★★★

Here, shrouded in mystery, is the history of a lost civilisation. My quest was to lead directly to the great Pyramids of Egypt, the most important surviving stone monuments of a highly advanced ancient civilisation. They are still controversially studied to unlock the mystery of the origins of mankind and long-lost civilisations.

Not surprisingly, at the end of the 1990s one can find a number of Internet sites that sum up the Great Zimbabwe ruins in half a page. The general consensus goes a little like this: the Shona-speaking ancestors of today's Zimbabweans had built these edifices during the thirteenth and fourteenth centuries. Excavations in 1929 by the archaeologist Gertrude Caton Thompson backed this up, as she discovered mainly artefacts of local Bantu origin.

The conclusion is right, because for many centuries the site of the current ruins of Zimbabwe were used, and possibly rebuilt on the original sites, by local people. We do know that stone structures can last many thousands of years, occupied by subsequent generations. Egypt and the Babylonian empire are just two examples where many buildings were occasionally even rebuilt by later generations that clearly did not have the same skill and understanding, nor the reasons for building these magnificent structures in the first place. There are several pyramids in Egypt that have proved to be of a much later period than those of Giza, and of much inferior building style.

* * *

But first, before returning to the ancient Egyptian connection, the great mystery of the ruins of Zimbabwe lay before me.

As we shall see later, to understand these ruins and the history of East Africa in the context of its distant past one needs to solve a puzzle that goes like a thread through fascinating ancient civilisations. We have isolated accounts of these, mainly from the Greeks who in turn received their stories from the Egyptians, going back into the remote past – way beyond 10,000 BC.

But what really had the builders of Zimbabwe in mind? Were they connected in any way to the ancient Nubian empire, and that of Azania? We know of these only from oral tradition in Africa, and later from the Arab traders who ventured along the coast from the Red Sea to the Cape of Good Hope.

II

REDISCOVERY

After we stoned the city of the Strange Ones, a hundred generations went by.

From The Blot of Zima-mbje, *Bantu tale*

The examination of the Great Zimbabwe ruins by the German geologist Carl Mauch in 1872 marked a new development for the mysterious ruins. These immaculate stone structures have been the subject of much speculation and expert archaeological excavation in the past 80 years. Africa has many mysteries, starting in antiquity around 10–9 BC on the Mediterranean coast and the great Egyptian civilisation. In particular, the Pyramids at Giza and the Sphinx are currently undergoing intensive research about their age and their actual function.

Like Egypt, Zimbabwe boasts an area that is scattered with stone structures built without mortar, although Zimbabwe's are not as elaborate as those in Egypt. The ancient Zimbabweans are said to have used these buildings for worship and astronomical observation. A fair amount of controversial material has appeared about the origin of the builders of the various ruins discovered in Zimbabwe.

One thing always struck me as rather odd. If the many gold-smelting spots discovered in the vicinity of the ruins were established by apparently resident Makanga

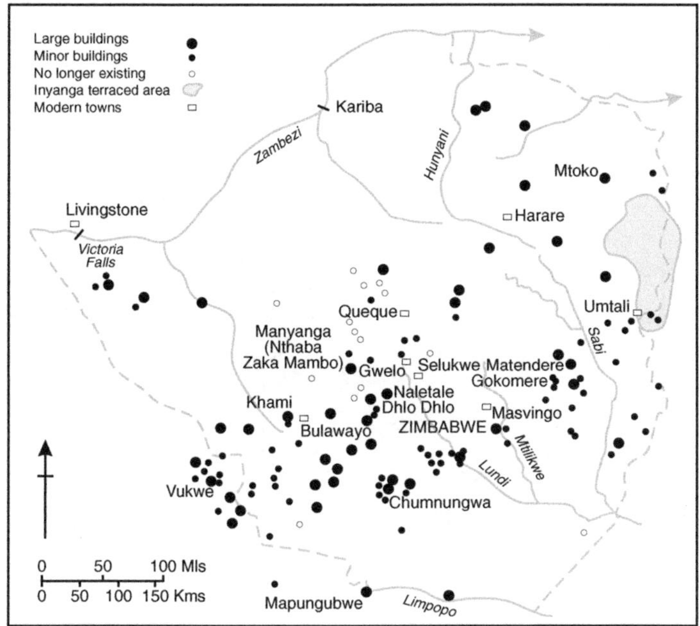

Zimbabwe's ancient settlements

kingdoms around the fifteenth century, how come so many Arab traders reported trade with the interior at a much more remote time?

In fact Arabian writers of the ninth and tenth centuries AD frequently mention the gold of Sofala (in present-day Mozambique); but to the western world this country was actually a blank spot until Portuguese explorers set sail around Africa on a mission to find the kingdom of Prester John, reportedly that of Abyssinia.

Let us take a closer look at some of the various excavations at Zimbabwe, and first at the rediscovery that took place on a hot afternoon in 1868.

Although the existence of the ruins was already known to the German missionary Rev. A. Merensky, he did not

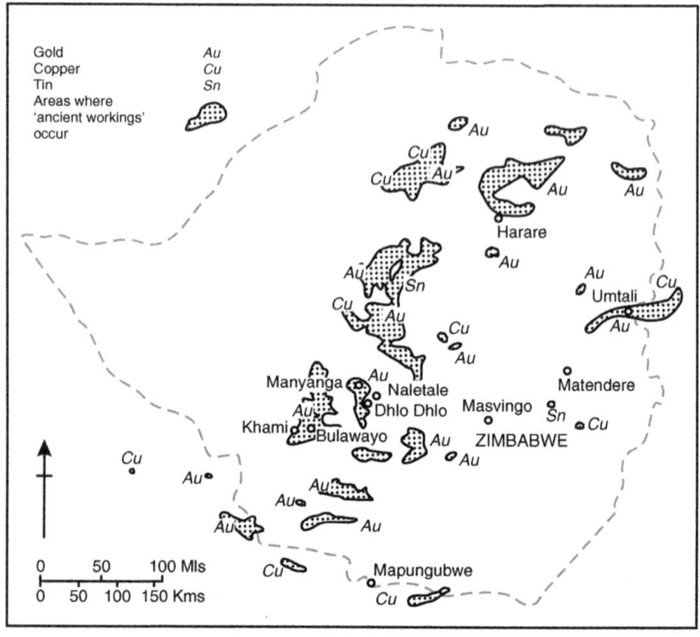

Zimbabwe's ancient metal-working sites

visit Zimbabwe himself. He spoke to travellers about the site, which was near his home at Louis Trichardt in the Transvaal (Northern Province in today's South Africa). Apparently he had heard of the many ruins from natives when they converted to Christianity at his mission.

An American hunter called Adam Renders (who might well have heard of these mysterious ruins from Merensky) finally saw the ruins in 1868, and returned there on several occasions until 1871. It is said that he in fact died within the vicinity of the ruins.

This did not make major news until Mauch – who was very probably in Merensky's confidence – went off by himself with a few carriers. He almost died of exhaustion in the bush after his helpers deserted him, and was picked

The Zimbabwe Bird found at the ruins – now the national emblem

up by Kalanga tribesmen. He remained with them as a prisoner until the middle of 1872. His release was possibly made easier by Renders living in the area at the time.

Mauch finally walked to Sena on the Zambezi river and eventually made his way back to the Transvaal. Thus

Cylinder found at Zimbabwe, now at South African Museum

Mauch became the first person to publish detailed accounts on Zimbabwe.

During the 1880s quite a few hunters lived in the area, although exploration of Mashonaland, by then under the rule of the powerful Matabele King Lobengula, was discouraged. Lobengula's kingdom came out of the great Monomotapa empire of the fifteenth century, which, as we shall see later, had established itself over a vast area.

Another important event took place in 1889, when Willi Posselt bought a soapstone bird and a carved cylinder from a chief at Zimbabwe and brought them south, where he sold them to none other than Cecil Rhodes, the founder of Rhodesia. The famous bird carvings are currently at

Groote Schuur House and the South African Museum, Cape Town. Without doubt the birds are a relic of the ancient past of Zimbabwe.

In 1891 Theodore Bent and his wife arrived in Mashonaland. He became the first archaeologist to survey the land and sites. His diggings and observations were published in his excellent and somewhat controversial book *Ruined Cities of Mashonaland*.

On his arrival, Bent found the ruins covered in vegetation, and he cleared the sites with the help of Bantus living in the area. Bent vividly describes several weeks of travelling on ox wagons through the green hills of Zimbabwe, encountering Makalanga tribesmen. His book has had a great effect on the theory of the origins of Zimbabwe, and his fascinating observations and evidence will be looked at later in the light of all other information.

Shortly after Bent returned to London, Sir John Willoughby, another Englishman, obtained permission to dig around the ruins in 1892. However, in the great Victorian tradition, while clearing the Valley ruins, at the same time he virtually destroyed important evidence on three smaller ruins.

Where ransacking is concerned, the name of R.N. Hall should be mentioned: he acted as a curator of the ruins in 1902 and completed the clearing and building of paths. Although to his credit he worked in great detail on numbering and naming the various sites, he used his own discretion and removed earth deposits, wiping out a large amount of evidence.

Now we enter the ruins and set eyes on their extraordinary architectural style.

The ruins

Bent and his party reached the mighty ruins of Zimbabwe on 8 June 1891. Without delay he hired local tribesmen to clear the immense site.

> I almost despaired getting rid of thick jungle which filled the large circular ruin, so that it was almost impossible to stir in it. What appeared at first sight to be a true circle eventually proved elliptical – a form of temple found such as at Marib, the ancient Saba and capital of the Sabean kingdom in Arabia.

The main features at the site have now been restored and make a great impression on any visitor. At the centre is the circular ruin known as the Great Enclosure, with its round tower on the edge of a gentle slope. Overlooking and quite imposing is the intricate fortress on the granite hill above, acting as the Acropolis of the ancient city.

The ruins are located at latitude 20° 16′ 30″ south and longitude 31° 10′ 10″ east, on the high plateau of Mashonaland about 3000 feet above sea level.

There is an extraordinary air of mystery about the ruins as one approaches the main site. I experienced a similar curiosity when visiting ancient Maya sites in the Mexican Yucatan.

There are various stone sites left around the vicinity of the Great Enclosure. The sight of this walled circular ruin with its round tower on the edge of a slope is spectacular in every sense of the word – every stone, bit by bit, carefully laid like the pieces of a puzzle, with a precision that would have required a high degree of architectural and building knowledge.

These remarkable buildings are built on granite and of granite with quartz reefs taken from a source a few miles distant. Significantly, no mortar was used in the various

View over Zimbabwe from hilltop Acropolis to Enclosure

buildings, yet the quality of the workmanship can be seen very clearly.

It was not until 1905 that modern scientific research took place, and it led again to disputed evidence as to the origins of Zimbabwe and its builders. David Randall-MacIver published a quite controversial account of his visit to the ruins and subsequently got into a typical academic argument as he dismissed outright Hall's less than careful excavations. Even 80 years later, various archaeologists differ about the prehistory of the Great Zimbabwe ruins.

Then, as if all this was not enough, the archaeologist Gertrude Caton Thompson went to re-examine the whole problem of dating the ruins. In her excellent account she finally concluded that Zimbabwe was an entirely local affair and that the products found during diggings were indeed of Bantu origin and dated to the tenth century AD. More precisely, she said:

> Examination of all the existing evidence gathered from every quarter still cannot produce one single item that is not in accordance with the claim of Bantu origin and the medieval date.

That is food for thought.

Certainly many clay pots and layers of previous inhabitants' huts were found on the site, but that does not prove that the original builders were from the Monomotapa empire as it came to its height in the fifteenth century. Her detailed scientific account on the ruins makes a good read, but strangely the excavations made her conclude: 'Zimbabwe is a mystery which lies in the pulsating heart of Africa' – not exactly definitive as to its origins.

This dating game continued throughout the twentieth century, with field work carried out by various archaeologists, but just when the age of sophisticated building began at Zimbabwe has still not been determined with accuracy.

Then in 1950 the curator of the Zimbabwe ruins, Mr Sanders, found a piece of wood built into a drain in the Temple. Apparently this was removed under the supervision of K. Robinson, the chief inspector of monuments. This undoubtedly raised hopes of giving a more accurate time of origin. Once the wall was opened up, two pieces of timber were found and a radiocarbon (carbon-14) test was carried out, proving that these pieces of wood had ceased to grow between AD 591 and AD 702.

The fact that these African sandalwood trees live many years after their heart wood stops growing was mentioned in Roger Summers' guide to Zimbabwe. Thus Summers and Robinson came to the conclusion that the walls of the Temple could not be earlier than AD 702.

From this evidence they simply concluded that the dates given by Bent and Hall, going back to Phoenician times, were effectively disproved.

In 1958 Sanders and Robinson did further excavations and stated that the Acropolis on the hill is older than the oldest part of the Temple. Most importantly, they claim that the Temple buildings themselves have been altered and rebuilt, so that what we see today is quite recent.

According to Sanders, a number of trenches were dug by Robinson in the Western Enclosure on the hill. There he found 'clear' evidence of five periods of occupation. Apparently the first ended and the second began during the fourth century AD and suddenly during the third period the first stone walls were built, around AD 1100, eventually leading to the fourth and richest period during the fifteenth century.

Summers goes so far as to say that some people feel disappointed that the old-fashioned romantic theories have not been upheld by the findings of archaeology, thus disposing of any possibility of great antiquity or any exotic civilisation.

Many anthropologists claim that all civilisations as remote as Zimbabwe were the result of isolated tribes who developed the building of their own edifices with little contact with the outside world.

Again we find great inconsistency, as in the 1960s a burial site was found near the Kariba Dam, and the Rhodes/Livingstone Museum carried out carbon-14 dating that placed the site between AD 680 and AD 800, effectively disproving a medieval date. The Kariba Dam is located in the north of Zimbabwe.

Here we have a good example of how easy it is to dismiss much evidence of an early civilisation when one does not see the bigger picture of a culture that possibly built these edifices for worship, protection and star-gazing.

In the Abbé Breuil's book *The Rock Paintings of Southern Zimbabwe* there is a rock painting from Zimbabwe (see page 35) depicting a man with beard, pointed shoes, armour and a helmet – strikingly similar to the Phoenician explorers. In fact Breuil's 'first school of thought' on southern Africa shows indications of a so called 'foreign' invasion several thousand years ago of 'Nilotic' origin such as the great civilisations of Egypt and Crete.

This is just one of many examples where there continues to be evidence from sometimes strange theories, but setting this in the context of the mystery of Zimbabwe's origins and that of many gold-smelting sites and other discoveries in East Africa, I beg to differ.

Near Arusha at Kilimanjaro in Tanzania, a discovery was made by a Tanganyika district officer in 1935. Ancient ruins and stone-walled houses with ancient terraces possibly used for irrigation were investigated by the famous Dr L.S.B. Leakey, who said that they were no older than about 300 years.

That ancient terraces and roads do exist all over East Africa is by now quite well known – although some 'experts' come up with a date no older than 300 years! – not to mention the northern Zimbabwe terraces of Inyanga, which have yet to be dated.

In his book *Lost Cities of Africa*, Basil Davidson did not accept the dating to the thirteenth to fifteenth centuries. It seems quite impossible that such large stone cities could only really be 300 years old when even the locals were not even aware of the location.

More importantly Axum (Aksum), the Abyssinian rulers' centre, was one of many trading places that were very probably connected to the mysterious Azania empire, of which we know very little.

One sign that could have ancient Phoenician and even Celtic links are the so-called 'cup marks' that were found at the ruins in Tanzania. Those marks have been found in Scotland, Malta and Ireland.

The mystery city of Engaruka is one of many large ancient cities in Africa that have not yet been explained. But through the quest to understand Zimbabwe we shall find a very ancient connection indeed.

Inscriptions have been found at Driekops Eiland on the Riet River in South Africa. It is the Ogam script in the Canaanite language, as used in the Sabaean kingdoms of Arabia around 1000 BC, according to Barry Fell of Harvard, who deciphered it. The Ogam script is known as a type of writing very much used then by sea traders.

The Enclosure

As we approach the ruins of the main circular Temple, another name for the Great Enclosure, it becomes apparent that these ruins are not ordinary. At first glance it seems the

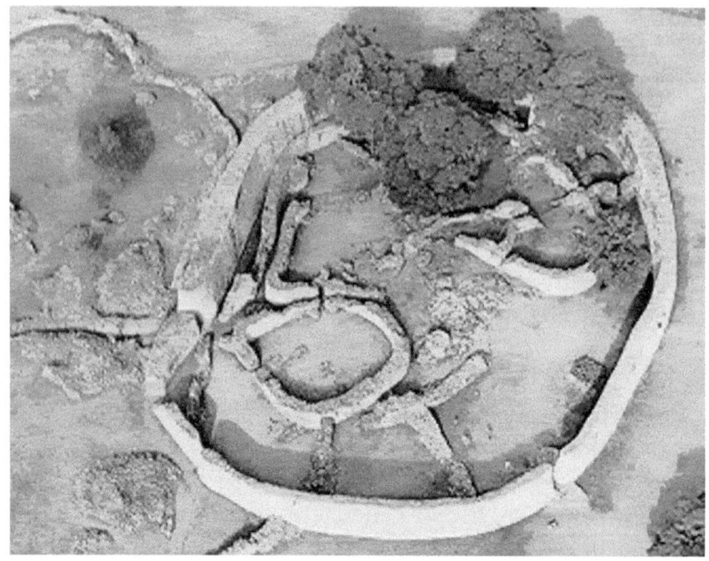

The Great Enclosure

architects of this building had rather carelessly drawn a great ellipse on the ground and built around it. The impression is that they got out of line, then left space for the odd doorway.

That this is not so can be seen by the detailed stone wall, each stone on the outer wall showing a chevron pattern facing the sun. As one walks around the great wall to the right of the main entrance, the great chevron pattern is even more impressive when viewed about 20–30 yards away from the wall – another striking feature that brings up further questions as to the reasons for making this pattern at this specific spot.

The great outer wall is an immense structure of stone masonry about 831 feet in diameter, with a maximum

Enclosure with chevron pattern

height of 31 feet at the side with the chevron pattern. The thickness reaches 19 feet at the base.

It has been estimated that over 15,000 tons of stone were used for the wall alone, and the equivalent at the Acropolis at the hilltop complex.

Not only did the original builders have superb skills in the organisation of a large labour force, but also the granite required splitting off in the surrounding countryside. Several quarry areas around the ruins west of the Temple or Great Enclosure show the immense task of carrying stones over a distance to the sites.

Apparently the builders were an unmechanised community. This is hard to believe since, as we will see later, the ancient Phoenician connection suggests that the builders would at least have known about sledges in order to move this amount of stone.

As one enters the North Entrance, one of the other main curious features is the so-called Parallel Passage, which even on a sunny day gives a gloomy feeling. Speculations have been made about religious processions or secret entry. Bent described it vividly:

> ... the great and astounding feature is the long narrow passage leading direct from the main entrance to the sacred enclosure, so narrow in parts that two people cannot walk abreast, whilst on either side of you rise the stupendous walls, thirty feet in height, and built with such eveness of courses and symmetry that as a specimen of the dry builder's art it is without a parallel.

The large blocks of cut stone used in Egyptian, Greek and Roman masonry must have been relatively easy to deal with in comparison to these small stones of rough granite.

After about 220 feet the passage ends in steps and then the ancients would have faced the Conical Tower. Remarkably, Bent found halfway down this passage an unexplained hole neatly executed through the thickest part of the wall, although there are similar tunnels at the hilltop Acropolis.

Even after Bent made his excavations it is agreed by many archaeologists that the two conical towers are a superb piece of work. Suspicions that these towers were hollow were disproved by Caton Thompson, who tunnelled beneath the foundation.

Strangely, many guesses have been made as to the function of these towers, and it remains a mystery. A royal kraal, for example, could have contained permanent initiation symbols like these towers. As we will see in later chapters, such symbols were also obviously connected to Phoenician

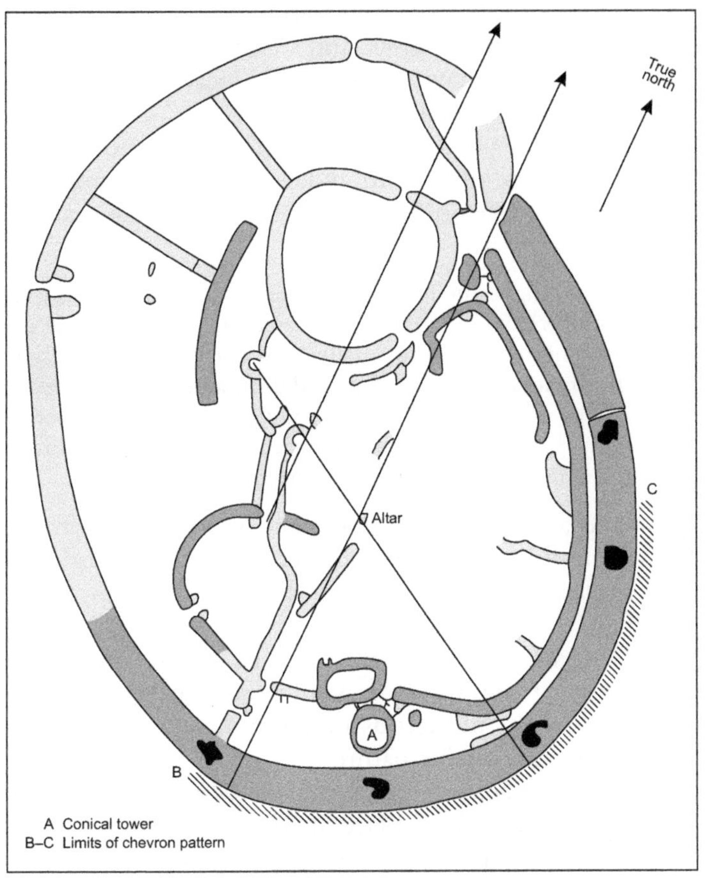

Plan of the Great Enclosure

phallic worship. The truth is that archaeology has not yet been able to produce any evidence as to the use of these towers, and oral Bantu tradition has strangely been silent about their function.

H.C. Woodhouse wrote various papers on the archaeology of southern Africa, and supports the view that Arab traders might have advised the local Karanga on the building technique.

But when we go back to Bent's observations, we will find answers that again indicate good reasons for the builders to have positioned these two towers at that particular spot.

> By digging to the foundations we were able to get very accurate measurements of [the towers], and found that the circumference of the smaller one corresponds exactly to the diameter of the big one, and the diameter of the big one is apparently equal to half its original height ... the battering of the big tower is carried out with mathematical accuracy, the slope of the curve being perfectly regular.

The ability of a civilisation to structure and measure these buildings undoubtedly points to religious and star observations. These towers did not have any use for defence or as a lookout.

Bent again gives a clue when he states: 'The religious purpose of these towers would seem to be conclusively proved by the numerous finds we made in other parts of the ruins of a phallic nature.'

Although Mauch mentioned in 1871 that he saw a sacrifice ceremony taking place, it corresponds to other Bantu tribes who were known to celebrate the spirits of their ancestors and looked upon the circular ruins as a sacred place long after the previous builders had vanished.

When we look closely at the Phoenicians' temple construction, we find many parallels between those in Zimbabwe and at Byblos: coins depict the tower or sacred cone within a temple.

The land surveyor R.M. Swan wrote a very detailed survey of the buildings and the surrounding country as

Coin of Byblos showing round tower

part of Bent's trip. He states in his chapter on the measurements and possible star observations:

> We could at first discover no reason for [the conical tower] being built in its peculiar position ... but it is in the middle of the space marked off by the two inner doorways, and the more easterly of these two doorways is at the point where the sun would appear when rising at the summer solstice when regarded from the central altar ... and the other doorway is at the point where the Chevron pattern on the outer wall terminates and that is at the part of the wall where the sun's rays would be tangential to its curve when rising at the same solstice.

Who were these star-gazers and heavenly builders? Some other major features come to mind, and again Swan points the way. Close to the great tower is the small one, and no reason for its position suggests itself. However, the relative proportions of the two towers are curious and indeed offer an explanation. In fact Swan says the diameter of the great tower seems to have represented the unit of measure in the construction of the curves of the outer walls, and of all the regularly curved inner walls in the Great Temple – and in all the other temples found in Zimbabwe today.

Strangely Swan then concludes in his exhaustive report on all the measurements of the various ruins

> … we do not suppose that it was intended to symbolise anything of an astronomical nature, it is extremely improbable that the builders of Zimbabwe had any notion of mathematical astronomy, for their astronomy was purely empirical, amounted merely to an observation of the more obvious motions of the heavens.

We will see later that this is far from the truth, although when he wrote this at the end of the nineteenth century, many facts that we understand today about the ancient civilisations were not known.

As we will see at another smaller ruin called Matindela, star observation was indeed a most important aspect of life in ancient Zimbabwe.

Between the Hill Complex and the Temple Enclosure lie the many dry-stone enclosures that make up the so-called Valley complex. This has been occupied over many centuries by the various Bantu kingdoms and the style is quite mixed, indicating that these valley ruins are likely to have been dwellings. There is evidence that these buildings were indeed made long after the original building style.

Possibly the best indication of the ongoing dispute about the origins of Zimbabwe lies at the so-called Maund Ruins in the valley which were excavated by Caton Thompson in 1929. Her theories of the Zimbabwe culture were essentially based on this dig. How this site, which has a slightly similar style but is vastly inferior in quality of execution to the Temple Enclosure, can be compared is clearly open to question.

The Acropolis Hill

It has been said that the location on top of the hill amongst gigantic granite boulders was determined by the climate: it is a place sheltered from the south-east winds in the winter months.

As one approaches up the ancient ascent, the hill gives an awesome feeling. It would have been a site of great importance, a fortress possibly to protect the ancient foreign builders from local invaders.

It is believed that this is the oldest part of the great ruins of Zimbabwe, and it is here that the soapstone birds, now the national emblem, were found.

Further suggestions have been made that between the thirteenth and fifteenth centuries this complex was the base of a Shona–Karanga civilisation. But of course the original builders of this enormous complex go back many centuries further.

The final climb up the hill leads into a very narrow passage between massive rocks, as if the weight of these boulders was used to intimidate.

The most prominent feature of the maze of walls in this labyrinth of rocks is the immense wall on the right overlooking the valley: it is about 25 feet high. On top of this wall are little turrets and monoliths. Bent describes one interesting aspect of a large semicircular space below the monolith platform, in the centre of which stood an altar covered with a thick coating of cement. Forming as it does the largest level space on the Acropolis, Bent reckons it was used as an *agora*, where a crowd could have been addressed for religious celebrations on a large scale.

We have already seen that the altar at the Temple Enclosure was aligned to a significant point with the conical tower for the observation of the summer solstice. The points marked B and C on the plan (page 19) show the extent of the chevron pattern ornament – a pattern that is known as the symbol of fertility – and it extends along the part of the wall which receives the rays of the sun when rising at summer solstice.

Swan observes similar means of viewing the summer solstice at the east end of the hill complex. Here a small part of a patterned wall was found, receiving the rays of the sun at summer solstice.

At the opposite end the Western Enclosure, with its great curved wall topped by the monoliths, faces the setting sun at the winter solstice. Swan goes on to make a most striking point: if we suppose an altar was placed here, we have an eminence fifty feet true north of the altar, a tall monolith which would enable the meridian transits of northern stars to be observed from the altar, and a line drawn from this altar towards the setting sun at the winter solstice would seem to have passed through the middle of the line of towers and monoliths.

That said, we are now on our way to finding the true nature of a civilisation deeply involved in star watching, possibly related to its priestly ceremonies. But it was also a civilisation of great gold traders. The hill complex revealed a gold furnace which has been used for many centuries.

To appreciate the style of walling between the immense boulders, one can see at the entrance of the Covered Passage an area that shows the original condition of the doorway. From the stone, delicately placed without mortar to blend in with the giant rocks leaping out, it can be seen

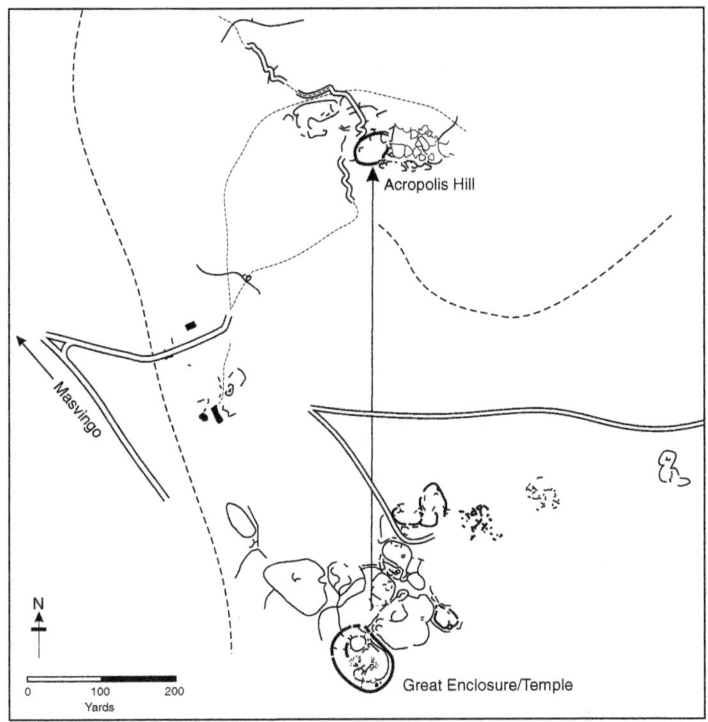

Overall site map from Enclosure to hill complex

that the original builders were engaged in extending the boulders upward and sideways.

This area is recognised as the earliest period of Zimbabwe building, quite different from the daga huts that followed during the thirteenth to fifteenth centuries at the height of Monomotapa kingdom.

Again, we find ourselves at a crossing point to uncover the mystery of these magnificent ruins. The Eastern Enclosure of this hill complex gives a clue to what many travellers and local tradition reported as being a most sacred place – a place that has been badly damaged by treasure seekers and subsequent inhabitants.

Today one can only try to imagine what this Enclosure looked like. In the centre would have been a small granite platform with a lower platform featuring great soapstone bowls such as can be seen in Bent's *Ruined Cities of Mashonaland,* where he describes in great detail the many finds during his excavations. In front there is a balcony which in turn leads to another platform which would have featured pillars on which the birds stood.

The various birds have different patterns, such as zigzag lines and circles, carved on their wings. They look in different directions. Were they the watchers over the heavens that seemed to have such importance for the builders of Zimbabwe?

Apart from the bird figures, soapstone carvings in geometric designs and strange-looking, stalk-like objects covered with gold leaf would have featured here. We see here the importance of the bird and its possible connection with Egypt and the Sabaean times.

But the Acropolis Hill complex was also strategically placed for defence of the civilisation that came here to build, trade and observe the stars.

Matindela – a mirror image

In the quest to answer the mystery of Zimbabwe and the many gold-smelting sites on the east coast, there is another ruin that I needed to see first-hand, that of Matindela.

Of the many ruined settlements that are scattered around Zimbabwe, Matindela is of particular interest to the question of finding out what the original builders actually had in mind.

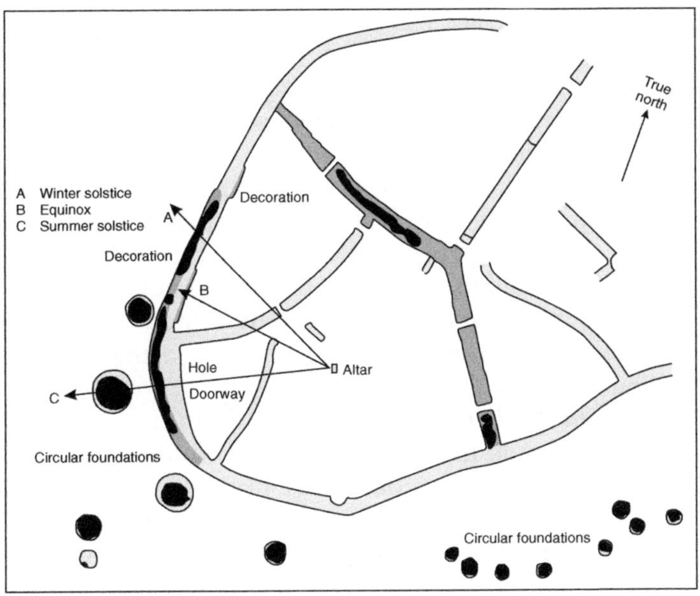

Plan of Matindela

Although Matindela is believed to have been built during a time of decadence, when the methods of building had fallen far behind the original refined standard, there are still some remarkable features.

The south-eastern wall has been built very thick – over 11 feet. Patterns laid into the wall again show a striking decoration, leading to the assumption that this was indeed a temple.

Looking west from the altar there is a herring-bone pattern running over the main entrance. Where it stops, an entirely different dentelle pattern starts two feet below.

On the top of the thick wall are holes which would have carried monoliths similar to those at the Great Zimbabwe ruins. Thus there is again an indication that we are looking at star-gazers and a cult who worshipped the sun.

From the place where an imaginary altar was located, a straight line passes through the doorway and a circular foundation not far from the main entrance (see map, page 27), a point where the ancients would have observed the summer solstice.

We can try to imagine the high priests, familiar with the ancient phallic belief of nature worship, ceremonially observing the planets, effectively acting like a modern astronomical observatory without the latest technology.

A loophole in the wall above the dentelle pattern probably served to direct sunlight from the setting sun to this altar at some celebration.

Point B, where the straight line hits the inner wall decorations, would have been the vernal equinox observation. In other words, this point to the observers would have the celestial equivalent of the Greenwich meridian on Earth.

A further line A can be drawn reaching from the altar in the centre of Matindela for the observation of winter solstice.

We have further proof of the importance the sun had for the people living here, which Swan describes:

> The construction of the doorways at Matindela is remarkable. They have been originally made of considerable width, and then been narrowed very much by square masses of masonry … The direction of the doorways also seems to have some meaning … for three of them look East 25 degrees North and four East 25 degrees South thus corresponding to the direction of the sun rising and setting at the solstices.

But what is it about the sun that in many folk customs took on such importance?

In Egypt there were several festivals in honour of Ra or Re, the Sun. The Greek writer Plutarch states that a sacrifice was performed to him on the fourth day of every month. This is related in the books of genealogy of Horus, by whom that custom was said to have been instituted. So great was the veneration paid to the Sun, that the Egyptians burnt incense to him three times a day – resin at his 'first rising, myrrh when in the meridian, and a mixture called kuphi' at the time of setting.

Another festival in honour of the Sun was held on the 30th day of Epiphi, so called birthday of Horus' eyes when the Sun and the Moon were in the same right line with the earth; Plutarch goes on to state

> about the winter solstice, they lead the sacred cow seven times in procession around her temple: calling this the searching after Osiris, that season of the year standing most in need of the Sun's warmth.

The local traditions that followed in the Mashonaland kingdoms did not show any of these star-observing qualities, for whatever reason, although Mauch reported the natives performing rainmaking rituals at the ruins at the time of his arrival in 1871.

As we shall see later, when the Portuguese finally arrived in the fifteenth century we find that no reference is made to any star worship being performed.

It is the long-overlooked ruins of Matindela that could well be the key to what the builders of Zimbabwe meant by observing the stars, by trying to leave a hidden message behind. Virtually no writing has been found but there are indications on a fragment which forms part of a large bowl that may represent Sabaean inscriptions similar to those used on Phoenician vases.

Whatever the inscriptions mean, our best bet to find the meaning of the buildings and the curious positions of the doors at Matindela is to look at the sky.

If standing near the centre or altar of Matindela facing the chevron pattern wall there are a number of circular foundations visible in front of the wall outside the enclosure.

If we assume that the high priests or those star-gazers used this site as an important landmark to observe the yearly cycles, they would almost certainly have a had a purpose for marking the circular foundations. Until now nobody has offered any reason for the use of these foundations.

When we look more closely at the map and that of the southern hemisphere night sky, it becomes strangely apparent that there is some sort of map mirrored from the heavens down on to the ground. This is strikingly similar to the Egyptians' accurate alignment of Giza with the Orion belt.

Although we do not have a pyramid to speak of, the curious fact remains that, when one mirrors the foundations, the ancient people would have looked at the night sky from the southern hemisphere towards north.

Swan's assumption could well be correct:

> the stars which were observed at Zimbabwe seem all to have been northern ones, and the builders of these temples probably acquired the habit of observing these stars in the northern hemisphere.

There is yet another strange remark by Bent as to the function of the circular foundations. Describing them as a stepped platforms used as dwellings is too easy an answer, since the line of the summer solstice lies directly in the middle of one of the larger circular foundations.

What could they be? When observing the night sky the ancients would have seen not only the ever prevalent Orion belt, but above it (looking north) the next compact grouping containing many bright stars, most notably Sirius, the brightest star of all.

The star Sirius, or Alpha Canis Majoris, is the brightest in the entire sky and one of the closest to the sun. It was identified by the ancient Egyptians as the celestial counterpart of their goddess Isis. (The name Sirius is related to the Greek for 'sparkling' or 'scorching'.)

This constellation thus mirrors the foundations found around the pattern wall of Matindela – a fitting celebration for the high priests, who could well have used Sirius as a major landmark for their astronomical observations. At first sight this looks to be the case. However, as we shall see later, by projecting the skies as the ancient people would have observed them at the summer solstice hundreds of years ago, we might then find a time when Zimbabwe may have in fact been settled.

The ruins of Matindela are without a doubt the remains of a temple correctly positioned for the observation of the heavens – but in which epoch is not quite clear yet.

III

THE SEA PEOPLE

There is nothing new under the sun.

attributed to Solomon

Amongst the many curious objects unearthed at the various Zimbabwe ruins were the famous birds, and phallic symbols such as soapstone beams, suggesting an early Semitic civilisation.

A Roman coin of the Emperor Antoninus Pius, dated AD 138, was found in an ancient shaft seventy feet deep near Umtali. Although such a find has been dismissed by many archaeologists as a possible link between the ruins and an ancient past well before Christ, it does say something important about the gold miners who worked at Umtali.

Either the Arabs brought this coinage up the East African coast, or the builders of Zimbabwe already had a well-established trading link using gold in exchange for Roman coins, although such an exchange is difficult to imagine.

One of the great finds is a wooden platter which was found in a cave 10 miles from the Zimbabwe ruins. In the middle is a carved figure of a crocodile, and the rim of the plate is a simple representation of the zodiacal characters such as Aquarius, Pisces, Cancer, Sagittarius and Gemini as well as Taurus and Scorpio.

Most remarkably there are figures of the sun and moon, a group of three stars, a triangle and four slabs with triangular punctures with two shown in reversed positions.

Again we find our quest to understand Zimbabwe thrown back in time to the ancient Egyptians. Clemens of Alexandria tells us about the customs '... of carrying gold figures in the festivals of the Gods'. They were two dogs, a hawk – is that the meaning of the famous Zimbabwe bird? – and the ibis. The dogs represented the hemispheres, the hawk the Sun, and the ibis the Moon.

Furthermore a number of beads that are related to Ptolemaic Egypt and pre-medieval India were also excavated.

Ingot moulds of soapstone in form of an X, such as were used by the Phoenicians in Britain, were also found, as were soapstone birds similar to those of Assyria, where they were used in the worship of Astarte, the Assyrian equivalent of Venus.

A number of phallic symbols were found, consistent with the phallic cult of nature. These are quite a find, indicating evidence of a link going back to at least 1000 BC.

Was it an early civilisation that decided to settle in the hills of Zimbabwe – a people well accustomed to seafaring and trading?

We can see the ancient Bantu people possibly conquered by a people of seafaring engineers, astronomers, architects and miners from the north.

We can see these invaders, exploiters of the rich gold mines, possibly destroyed 1000 years later by decadence, by the decline of their power over slaves and by the emergence of merchant Arabs who exploited the slave trade even further.

Finally came the Portuguese, around 1498, by which time many generations of Bantus had built important empires in the location of the mysterious Great Zimbabwe ruins.

But where exactly did the Sea People, as the Phoenicians are often called, come from, and what was their mission?

Ships of gold

It has been suggested that the gold for King Solomon's Temple came from Zimbabwe, since the mines are only about 200 miles from Sofala, which was famous for its gold exports in King Solomon's time. There is indeed evidence of a road leading into the interior from this port.

It could well mean that the ships built at Ezion-geber ('... and King Solomon made a navy of ships built at Ezion-geber', 1 Kings 9:26) were used for trade down the African coast and on to India.

Again I quote from 1 Kings 10:22: 'Once in three years came the navy of Tharshish, bringing gold, silver, ivory and apes, and peacocks.' The sea voyages along the east coast of Africa would have been easier with the monsoons, the trade winds of the Indian Ocean. In fact it is quite possible that Zimbabwe was part of a Sabaean empire – but only one of many destinations for Solomon, and quite likely part of a worldwide trading network reaching to Asia and even all the way to South America. In Mexico we see unmistakably carved Bantu heads of the so-called Olmec civilisation: where they came from is still not known.

The trading link of King Solomon (the son-in-law of a Pharaoh) with Hiram of Tyre may well have been a key element for the large shipments of gold needed to further Solomon's great building projects in Jerusalem, such as the

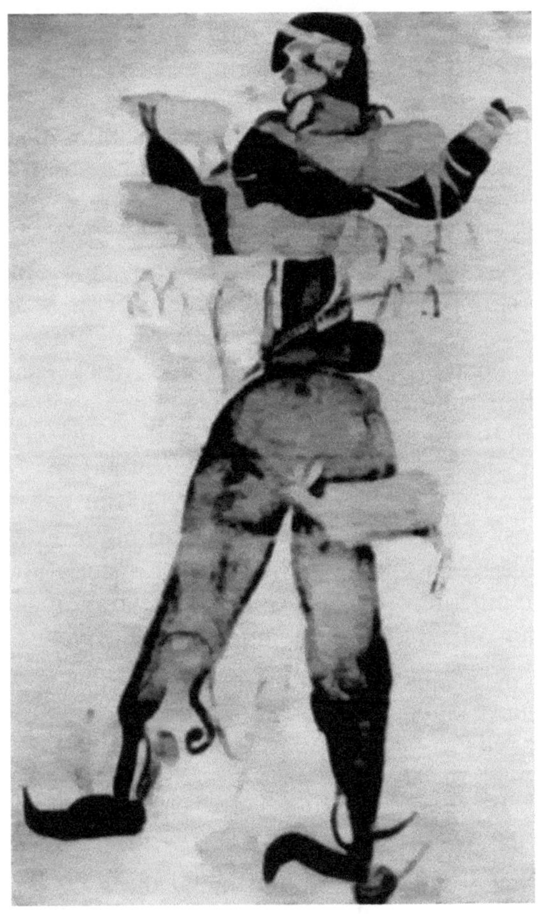

Man of Chamawara: rock painting of possible Phoenician explorer

palace and Temple of Jehovah. All this was achieved during his reign, around 966–926 BC.

At the same time the Phoenicians developed the most powerful autonomous city-states in the Mediterranean, their main port cities being Tyre, Byblos and Sidon. The collapse of Cretan commercial power gave the Phoenicians commercial success trading along the north African coast to the coast of Spain and all the way to Britain.

Carthage on the north African coast became an important trading port and possessed a fleet and army to become protector of the western Mediterranean empire. Much else is known on the Phoenicians' activities beyond the Red Sea.

It is through Greek sources via Herodotus that we gather more evidence of the achievements of Phoenician sailors. We hear that in the service of Pharaoh Necho around 600 BC '... they sailed round Africa having the sun on their right hand'. This all happened about 2100 years before Bartolomeu Diaz and Vasco da Gama were to rediscover the sea route for Europeans in 1498.

So when the Phoenicians departed on their excursions to cross the seas, they colonised various countries such as Greece. We again see an interesting aspect of their invaluable contribution to seafaring and boat building in Gardner Wilkinson's *Ancient Egyptians*, where he says

> ... the people to whom the art of navigation was most indebted, who excelled all others in nautical skill, and who carried the spirit of adventure far beyond any nation of antiquity, were the Phoenicians.
>
> Those bold navigators even visited the coast of Britain in quest of tin.

What about the gold and metal trade that is so clearly linked with Zimbabwe's past? Hundreds of gold-smelting sites have been discovered in Zimbabwe, reaching to what is today the northern part of South Africa.

The importance of gold goes back to the Egyptian dynasties who, as a centre of trade from earliest times, used the precious metals to great effect.

It is believed that the Phoenicians acquired the knowledge of working the mines from the Egyptians, who were in constant search of precious metals. Expeditions departed from Phoenicia, and we see the occupation of Sardinia, where the Phoenicians worked copper mines on the south-western portion of the island.

This great nation of navigators and traders was at its zenith around 1000 BC and colonised many parts of the world in that remote time, leaving traces of writing, stone buildings and mines behind them.

Two thousand years before Christ, large migrations had taken place, extending from the borders of Egypt deep into the Jordan valley. The tribes that conquered the Canaanites and Philistines were Hebrews, Phoenicians, and then Syrians.

The lands on the north African and Middle-Eastern shores of the Mediterranean witnessed a great exodus, but most remarkably the Phoenicians occupied only a small proportion of the land surrounding those great city states such as Sidon, Tyre and Byblos (in the area now known as Lebanon). In contrast, they developed the arts of seafaring and trading, looking towards the horizons.

The Phoenicians had no rivals in the art of mining for commercial purposes, and Zimbabwe must have been one of many outposts of their empire. Among their other colonies were the Aegean islands, Sardinia, Syria, north Africa and later Carthage, founded around the ninth century BC.

In the wider context we can say that Phoenician trading linked the entire world. For it is believed that the Phoenicians eventually sailed to the shores of South America. Writers on the ruins in Mexico have pointed to evident traces of Chaldean workmanship and characters, which were closely linked to the Phoenician language and religion.

It is beyond the scope of this book to go further into the disputed sea voyages that the Phoenicians are supposed to have made, but it is clear from Herodotus' account that they indeed circumnavigated Africa and traded in West Africa.

The importance of precious metals is described vividly by Strabo and Pliny when they say that the Sea People worked the British tin mines, which were remarkably rich. Indeed, so valuable were they that Strabo tells us of a case where a Tyrian captain, followed by Roman ships when near the Cassiterides (as Britain was known to the Romans), preferred to run his ship upon rocks rather than allow a rival nation to learn the secret of a safe approach to the tin-producing coast.

The first extensive mining operations of the Phoenicians were very probably started in Cyprus.

No doubt the earliest mining operations of which we have any record of were conducted by the Egyptian kings of the Fourth, Fifth and Twelfth Dynasties in the region extending between Suez and Mount Sinai. Their shafts were laboriously excavated in the rocks (Brugsch, *History of Egypt*). However, Spain, where silver was found in great abundance, was one of the richest of the Tarshishes of the world.

In addition the manufacture of linen, wool, cotton, metals, glass and silk was one of the great assets that Phoenicia used in its trading power. But nothing surpassed the importance of gold and other precious metals. The lands of Ophir, so often mentioned, may have been in East Africa. The fact that King Solomon and Hiram of Tyre were close allies for 20 years may be relevant: not only was King Solomon master of the port of Ezion-geber on the Red Sea, but he also controlled the trade routes along the Syrian valley via Aleppo and Tadmor.

Large amounts of gold were needed, and the Mediterranean coasts did not supply this quantity. The Phoenicians were forced to look beyond the Red Sea.

Temple and symbol builders

Further pointers of a link between the Phoenicians and a culture in Zimbabwe are the form of several forts or temples built in the Mediterranean – namely in Malta, Cyprus, Sicily and Sardinia.

A circular temple similar to the Great Enclosure of Zimbabwe can also be found at Marib in Yemen. At Nauraghe in Sardinia is a tower with a pointed cone constructed without mortar.

It is believed that these were temples built by the ancient Phoenicians. Indeed, as many as two hundred such sites have been discovered in Sardinia. The importance of this link with the early builders of Zimbabwe is that in Sardinia the great courts of the Nauraghe-type structures, in which some kind of worship took place, are of circular character and 'open to heaven'.

The fact is that near the conical towers were altars such as we see in Zimbabwe, and so-called 'high places' where the Phoenicians practised their religious ceremonies. Interestingly, the Nauraghe-type structures of Sardinia are generally found on the slopes of mountains or the summits of hills.

The presence of monoliths and of rough blocks of stone which are doubtless phallic emblems signifying nature worship, both found in the Nauraghes of Sardinia and at Great Zimbabwe, points again to a more ancient link with people who came to Zimbabwe from the north of Africa.

C.P. Thile mentions in his *La Religion Phoenicienne*:

> The most ancient religion of Syria, of Phoenicia, and of Canaan consisted in the fundamental idea of fruitful marriage of heaven with earth, or vivifying mysterious action of fire in the waters of the celestial ocean.

Conical stones such as are still visible in Zimbabwe and even huge rough blocks of stone became the expressions of this religion – in an idol form. What does the very ancient phallic worship have to do with Zimbabwe?

All peoples of the world worshipped the sun under a selected name. Everywhere a sun god was adored. Darkness, depression and the lowering of temperature following the setting of the sun were signs of the influence of negative forces. Not surprisingly, the sun was looked upon as the most powerful and beneficial spirit of all.

Solomon, for example, built a high place for the worship of the sun (Chemosh: see 1 Kings 11:7), and the kings of Judah, one after another, practised the same form of worship, even dedicating horses to the sun. The Egyptians, Persians and ancient Hindus all worshipped the sun.

Baal, the god of the Canaanites, identical with Yahweh, the Hebrew tribal god, was a solar deity. The Egyptians had a most powerful sun god: Amon-Re.

People looked to the heavens and accordingly built temples for sacrifices, ceremonies and star observation – astronomy being of great importance to the ancients.

Columns of stone were consecrated to Baal, as referred to in the Old Testament. The great temple of Tyre, which was constructed by Hiram, shows columns of jasper. More evidence of precious metal as part of that culture is at Cadiz in Spain, where the columns were made of copper.

Apart from the stones and buildings without mortar, the emblems of the Phoenicians included the conical towers – a serpent symbol meaning the sun. Motion and life on each side of the conical tower were implied.

It is here that we need to examine Bent's great finds at Zimbabwe of various soapstone birds perched on tall soapstone columns. From the point where they were found, they would appear to have decorated the outer wall of the semicircular temple on the hill. The conclusion he draws is that the birds represent hawks or vultures and that they evolved out of some sacred symbolism of which these birds were the embodiment.

As mentioned in the beginning of this chapter, there appears to be little doubt that these birds are closely akin to the Assyrian Astarte or Venus, and represent the female element in creation. The Phoenicians of course used similar birds, which were often represented as perched on Astarte's shrines. Phoenician coins found in Cyprus show a pedestal as the central object, with a dove sitting on the top.

There is plenty of evidence of the use of bird symbolism deep into ancient Egyptian times, where the vulture was emblematic of Urania, a year, or a mother.

In terms of the phallic cult of nature, these birds are interesting as they signify incubation.

Again, in Egypt, birds on pedestals have been found, particularly in the curious zodiac of Dandarah showing the bird on a pillar with the crown of Upper Egypt on its head. Similar smaller figures were also found at Zimbabwe.

Although Dr Charles Owen's *Essay Towards a Natural History of Serpents*, which asserts that the adoration of animals originated with the ancient Egyptians, may well be based on dubious findings, there is no doubt that these Egyptians were responsible for the extension and development of animal worship to a remarkable degree.

They represented many animals, including bulls, goats, dogs and monkeys. Birds too were worshipped: the pigeon was consecrated to their equivalent of Venus, the eagle to Jupiter, the cock to Esculapius, the owl to Minerva. To all of these animals they erected elaborate temples.

It is still not clear why the various relics found were dismissed by archaeologists. This is interesting, since none of the subsequent Bantu states, particularly that of

Monomotapa, practised with these emblems unless we simplify the assumption made by Tom Huffman. Remarkably he states:

> ... the symbolism and probable function of the Zimbabwe birds can be understood in terms of Shona beliefs. Birds, and particularly eagles, were seen as messengers to and from ancestral spirits and between men and God ... it is possible that the carved birds from Great Zimbabwe were metaphors for the spirits of departed kings.

It seems that the phallic symbols discovered at the Great Zimbabwe have had a much greater significance than has previously been accepted. The fact that pillars were erected at specific points in these ruins as previously mentioned clearly shows a phallic symbolism that goes well beyond ceremonies of departed kings.

Declining Phoenicia

The Phoenicians were greatly influenced by the ancient Egyptian sun worship and they in turn traded and mixed with the north African Nubian states and the Aksumites, the people of Abyssinia.

At the tail end of the Egyptian Twentieth Dynasty around 1000 BC, the Nubians based around the area of present-day northern Sudan posed a constant threat and the Abyssinians on the Horn of Africa no doubt had trading contacts with the Phoenicians.

To Europe, the lands of east Africa were *terra incognita* – or rather the unknown continent. After the Phoenicians fell, Arab traders took over these coastal waters as far as Mombasa, establishing trade in metal and slavery.

The Phoenicians, having navigated across the seas and exploited gold mines in many countries, no doubt had an influence on Great Zimbabwe – on its architecture, its ceremonies and the meaning of star observation.

Around 332 BC Tyre ceased to be a city and the decline of Phoenicia was already greatly accelerated a hundred years earlier, not long after we see it verified in the words of Ezekiel (27:31–36):

> And they shall weep for thee in bitterness of soul with bitter mourning,
> And lament over thee saying, Who is there like Tyre, Like her that is brought to silence in the midst of the sea?
> When thy wares went forth out of the seas thou filledst many people, Thou didst enrich the kings of the earth with thy merchandise and thy riches.
> In the time that thou wast broken by the seas in the depth of the waters, The merchants that are among the peoples hiss at thee;
> Thou art become a terror and thou shall never be any more.

This was the end of the most adventurous seafarers the world had ever seen.

Then silence – at least in Europe. Centuries of Arab trading expansion along the African coast followed, whilst these great buildings fell into decay until Europe emerged from the Dark Ages.

The arrival of the Portuguese at the beginning of the sixteenth century gives us the first written accounts that shed some light on the mystery of these ruins.

IV

THE PORTUGUESE CONNECTION

> Upon the gate of this monument is an inscription which the Moors and learned men who have visited the place are not able to understand.
>
> *De Barros*

Early Portuguese records show references to 'Zimbabwe'. However, doubts remain as to whether the Portuguese ever reached as far as the interior: these are based on the lack of written sources from the early Portuguese explorers who circumnavigated Africa as the first European sea power.

As we shall see, early Portuguese exploration all along the East African coast and the establishment of settlements required them to penetrate further into the wild interior, which was mainly known to Arab slave traders at the time.

In the 1420s the Portuguese Prince Henry the Navigator decided to establish the greatest school of navigation not seen since the Phoenicians. For four decades his ships, with the final blessings of the Pope, made unbelievable progress along the West African coast. At Sagres he gathered the best mathematicians, astronomers, cartographers, cosmographers and shipbuilders.

He ordered the collection of the finest maps and charts, which had not been seen for many centuries, in order to explore and conquer the treacherous winds and waters of the Atlantic. In fact it was said that the real mission King Henry had in mind was to find Prester John, that elusive emperor reputed since the dark ages as having a Christian empire somewhere in the east of Africa. Thus the race was on to navigate around Africa, where Ethiopia was now thought to have a Christian priest-king.

It is worth remembering that during the fourteenth century Africa was more or less unknown to Europeans. The church had plunged Europe into darkness for many centuries. This was at last about to change.

There is then a great possibility that for almost 2000 years, since the Phoenicians' sea venture around 600 BC, Africa had not been circumnavigated.

In Herodotus' histories we are indeed lucky to hear his account of Phoenician sailors who were apparently dispatched by Pharaoh Necho II of Egypt. Their route went southward down the Red Sea and along the East African coast, and back via the Pillars of Hercules (the Straits of Gibraltar) three years later.

That the Portuguese dared to challenge this is all the more curious considering that in medieval Europe the Atlantic was the *Mar Tenebroso*, the ocean of darkness. One can only vaguely imagine what terror this must have been for the mariners on the first ships making their way along the coast of West Africa. Conquering the unknown became the biggest challenge. Then the race was suddenly on to complete the blank spots of the incomplete maps of the world. The West African coast was entirely uncharted at the time.

Although the compass was in use, having reached Europe from China via the Arabs, the open sea posed formidable problems, and so did the coastal current.

It is highly likely that Henry, being apparently a Templar, had studied the various sciences himself and so would have had insight into long-buried knowledge of seafaring. It was not by accident that he gathered mathematicians and astronomers in order to ensure success for his expeditions.

Bartolomeu Diaz set sail for the south with two vessels in August 1486 and performed one of the most heroic deeds in seafaring history.

He was the gallant scion of a daring race of mariners. Before him, João Diaz had been the first to double Cape Boyador, and Deniz Diaz, who coasted Senegal and discovered Cape Verde, was among the foremost navigators.

By then it had become a custom to erect stone pillars as a record of discovery, and when Bartolomeu Diaz reached Pedestal Point on the West African coast, one of these was erected. Further along the coast down to the Orange river, further crosses were erected.

Algoa Bay was nearly the terminal point of the voyage of Bartolomeu Diaz. Here he erected a cross on the little island of St. Croix at the mouth of the Sundays river. At this point his crew made great difficulties in the light of the hardships and the unknown they had to face. They came to the end of their journey when they cast anchor at the mouth of Rio do Infanta, since known as the Great Fish River.

Later, on 25 November 1497, another explorer, Vasco da Gama, anchored in the Bay of St. Bras, and there encountered Bushmen. He then visited Algoa Bay and subsequently discovered the Natal coast.

Finally, on Monday, 22 January 1498 Vasco da Gama anchored his fleet in the Quillimi river at the mouth of the Zambezi, where he encountered Arab merchants. Da Gama gathered important information about the sea route to India and the route north to Mombasa and eventually Ethiopia.

The Monomotapa empire

Having now opened up the sea route from Europe to the Cape of Good Hope, the Portuguese set out to establish settlements in Africa on a serious commercial basis by building fortresses at Sofala and Quiloa in what is today's Mozambique.

Under the command of Don Francesco de Almeida, the first Viceroy of India, the Portuguese encountered the Monomotapa empire. Specific instructions were given to de Almeida in 1503 by King Manoel to commence practical operations on the East African coast.

The great Bantu empire of the Makalangas stretched between the Limpopo and Zambezi rivers, and extended along the Indian Ocean coast line for around one thousand miles; without doubt a powerful kingdom that came to its zenith in the fifteenth century.

Thus the fabled and disputed land of Ophir as described in the Bible lay before the Portuguese seafarers, who instantly made for this land awash with gold.

According to Wilmot's *Monomotapa (Rhodesia)*, Ophir was more a generic title refering to a rich commercial country, used in the same way as 'Tarshish'.

The latter name we know was given to various places such as in India at the Malabar coast and the south east coast of Africa and the Monomotapa empire.

It took some time for the Portuguese to make progress and establish missions, as the Moors (Arabs) had for many centuries controlled the eastern coast of the continent of Africa. In letters of the Jesuits from south-east Africa, seen at the Royal Library of Lisbon, it becomes clear that Portugal tried to obtain the riches of Monomotapa – such as gold – to support the great expenses of Portugal's colonisation of India and the spreading of the Christian faith.

Eventually the headquarters of Portuguese domination in the Indian Ocean were established at Goa in India. Still, the importance of Monomotapa was underlined by the building of an important fort at Quiloa, which was soon abandoned to make way for the centralised power based at Sofala. By about 1559 Sofala was the new gold coast. It became the most important port in the region.

Gold became the key word. An early sixteenth-century writing by Duarte Barbosa explains: 'in the interior (from Sofala) about 15 to 20 days journey is a great population named Zimbahoe.' He goes on: 'those Moors have a long time established themselves at Sofala because of great gold trade with the interior'.

His account goes further, claiming that large vessels came from Arabia to the port of Quiloa and smaller boats were used to go up the coast to Sofala.

But what about the great buildings of Zimbabwe in the interior? Very little is indeed written by the early Portuguese explorers since their main bases were along the coast and rarely did they venture into the dangerous interior.

The *Geographia dell'Africa* of Livio Sanuto of Venice, published in 1588, is considered one of the best accounts of how the King of Monomotapa reigned in what is today Zimbabwe:

> In the midst of the ancient mines that are known, Zimbaoe stands. Here is a fortress made of rough stones.

What this means is that even Sanuto was not an eyewitness to these amazing buildings, but took his information from the Moors. He goes on

> ... above the gate is an inscription after the fashion of an epitaph which no one has been able to understand. The word Zimbaoe signifies court and any place where the king of Monomotapa goes is called so ... these buildings are supposed to have been built to keep the gold.

> The mines now have not been worked for many years, by reason of the wars. The country has a circuit of about 3000 miles and there are many rivers in which there is gold.
>
> If the people sought in earnest after gold they would obtain it in great quantities, but they only take it to suit their fancy or give them the means of buying from foreigners.
>
> They worship a single god called 'Mozimo' and have no idols. They wear cotton clothing worked with gold thread. The King of Monomotapa holds sway to the Cape of Good Hope and great gifts are given to him by subject kings.

These were the early records of explorers not yet familiar with the interior and the centuries that pre-dated their arrival.

How did the so-called Monomatapa kingdom establish itself? Through the oral tradition and a paper written by the historian Dr D.P. Abraham and presented in Salisbury (Harare) in 1960, we can take a glimpse back in time. According to this paper, the ancestors of the Karanga people left their ancestral home on the shores of Lake Tanganyika during the ninth century AD and migrated southward with their cattle. After they crossed the mighty Zambezi river and the Munyati they encountered Tonga people, entering an area of wide plains, and also came across lighter-skinned hunters, the Masarwa.

Intermarriage took place and the descendants gradually spread over a large area as far south as the Limpopo river.

It is then claimed that over the years a clan called the Rozwi emerged as the dominant highly organised force. They established a religious centre on a hill with pleasant surroundings – what is now called Zimbabwe. They then commenced to build Zimbabwe, the great house of stone. This historical paper then states that from around 1250 onwards Sotho clans started to raid the north-western borders of the Karanga terrritory.

The Rozwi became very organised and established a system of tributary chiefs and appointed priests who ensured that the will of the ancestors added authority. A force to be reckoned with was a mambo or king called Mutota, who went on to conquer the country further north after having recognised the potential of further supplies such as salt. It is assumed that Mutota was given the praise name Mwene Mutapa (Master Pillager), which was corrupted to Monomatapa by the first Portuguese explorers.

Trade was of paramount importance to the Monomotapa kings. There is evidence that as early as 1320 they traded with the great ports, a vast network of Islamic cities all along the East African coast. In fact trade was so dynamic from the centre of Zimbabwe that traders from the Indian subcontinent even appeared.

Indian vessels, particularly from the Cambay region, made their way along the coast, whilst at the same time around 1414 the African coastal city of Malindi sent ambassadors to the court of the Chinese emperor, bearing with them a giraffe as a gift. In Davidson's 1959 account he says in return the Chinese Muslim admiral Cheng Ho (or Zheng He) sailed with a large fleet of ships to trade in the Indian Ocean.

How is it possible that such an influencial trading power declined within 200 years? A number of radiocarbon dates as published by Huffman and Vogel in 1986 date the Period 3 from the twelfth and early thirteenth centuries. That said, it would be easy to conclude that indeed a culture rose suddenly, building sophisticated stone structures that was astronomically aligned for some purpose. Later in this quest we shall be led to a different understanding of what the original builders really had in mind.

That Great Zimbabwe was significant as a centre of power is confirmed by its location on the hill, its central court. Interestingly, archaeologists disagree on the function of the buildings. For example, Peter Garlake claims the Enclosures as well as the smaller structures south of the great court are the houses of the ruling class. Garlake's theories are considered the most authorative based on his detailed studies. Huffman opposes this view, suggesting that the numerous grooved slots in these buildings were female symbols, and that these were the residences of the royal wives.

A more interesting theory is put forward by Huffman: that the Western Enclosure on the hill was a major living area, and in contrast the Eastern Enclosure at the other end of the hill may have been a religious centre. As the reader will recall, this is of course where the carved soapstone birds were found which became the Zimbabwe emblem today.

Huffman's theory is that the Shona religion was based on the spirits of former kings communicating with God on behalf of the nation, often through birds, which carry messages between heaven and earth. It was even claimed that each of the eight soapstone birds commemorates a different king.

The most fundamental question surrounding these beliefs must be why such distinguished scientists overlooked the fact that the walls of the buildings, chevron patterns and many relics found, including the conical tower, can have little to do with the use of such a major building as housing. However, they claim that this Enclosure was used as an initiation and ceremonial centre. Again, how could the Monomotapa court have abandoned these ceremonies by the time the first Europeans arrived? Is this not very plausible evidence that in fact a much earlier civilisation used these buildings?

In fact all over Zimbabwe there are many ruins and settlements which were built in the Shona tradition of clay-and-thatch houses. But only at Great Zimbabwe do we see a stone structure that is located strategically – or is there another reason?

We shall find further links pointing to an intriguing civilisation.

A Bantu's tale

We are now at the crossroads for the quest to find the date and the possible builders of Zimbabwe – a time that certainly goes way back beyond AD 700, surely not around the thirteenth century, as often believed.

The traditions of the people living at the time the Portuguese arrived strangely (although in many ways, not surprisingly) had little relationship to the surrounding buildings – edifices so magnificently constructed. It is difficult to imagine that a people would have lost the traditions of building, phallic sun worship and astronomical observations in a matter of three hundred years.

However, the pottery patterns used by the Makalanga when the Portuguese arrived did in some part resemble those of the Phoenicians. Still, the local people lived in huts in the vicinity of these great ruins without a written record or history of the past to tell, or so it is believed.

The puzzle of these ruins and many others in East Africa can only be solved by understanding the many connections that exist in ancient civilisations all the way up to Egypt before the birth of Christ.

In fact Egypt, the Mu empire, Azania, Nubia and Zimbabwe were all, in the great scheme of things, in contact via the Phoenicians' great maritime trading links.

An important book shedding light from the African view, by the respected Bantu anthropologist Wuzamazulu Mutwa and entitled *Indaba, My Children*, was published in 1964. It was banned in South Africa. Mutwa claims that the Zimbabwe area was inhabited by Bantu tribesmen who were descendants of an earlier invasion of people with red skin who actually built the fortress.

These are mysterious theories and are wrapped in local mythology: the hint we get is that again we see conquerors from an unknown land establishing buildings of great significance.

More intriguing is the story Orville Hope puts together in his book *6000 Years of Seafaring*. He states:

> … native historians of Bantu tribes in southern Africa state that Sea people came to the Zambezi river … possibly Sabeans including Canaanite or Egyptian priests, guides and slaves. They arrived long before the Arabs came among the Bantu people, they established control over the surrounding countryside … natives of the new Ma-Iti Empire who did not escape were taken as slaves.

This story may well be far-fetched but again it does give clues to the original builders. Hope continues:

> … The capital of Ma-Iti was on Lake Makarikari less than 100 miles from Plumtree (western Zimbabwe). The lake is gone, nothing remains but a large salt pan. The city is gone, only the foundations remain covered with soil and overgrowth. What remains is scattered Ogam script carved in Canaanite language and a few artefacts.
>
> Old swords, pieces of armour, battle axes and small trinkets or magic charms made of solid gold are in the possession of tribal historians and witch doctors. The relics are on occasion shown to the tribes but never to outsiders.

Whether Hope's vivid description of the ancient southern African history is correct can only be seen in the light of an understanding of the worldwide trading links of the Phoenicians.

In return, their knowledge of astronomy derived from Egyptian influence, and the importance of the gold exploitation that took place in and around the ruins of Zimbabwe points to a sophisticated trading civilisation.

If the Bantu tales themselves point to a Middle Eastern origin, then we find the claims of various scientific and archaeological reports of a culture no older than AD 700 far-fetched.

In fact the study of early African history is very much in its infancy. Even today it suffers from a lack of written records. It is only the Arab and Portuguese records that to some extent can provide some answers back beyond the fifteenth century. However, the Arab records are not easily accessible and are in terms of written evidence the most significant, as the Arabs have ventured along the coast of Africa since biblical times.

Despite that, it is the patient recording of oral traditions and the study of many rock paintings that reveal some interesting events in southern Africa.

Mutwa also points out that the Zulus and other tribes in the region possess relics such as swords from the days of the ancient Phoenician invaders. In fact, quite understandably, Bantu elders have kept many secrets from foreign invaders over hundreds of years.

The lack of European understanding of African beliefs has made assumptions about southern African history all the more confusing. Because of that lack of any written evidence, the Bantu tales were often dismissed.

In fact all points to a pink man's invasion, as outlined in Mutwa's tale. But are there any other pointers to an ancient civilisation?

★★★

I'm yesterday, I know today.

Egyptian Book of the Dead

It was at Christmas 1998 that I took a trip from Cape Town to the Indian Ocean seaside town of Muizenberg at False Bay. A sunny day, the heat of an African summer making people rush to the fine beaches along the coast.

Walking along the old colonial shopfronts at Kalk Bay to research further about the Zimbabwe ruins, I was lucky to spot an old book – or was it meant to be? An extraordinary account of various psychic episodes that took place in 1937, described in detail by H. Clarkson Fletcher, it gives us a further dimension and answers questions as to the origins of the builders of Great Zimbabwe.

During the the full moon of 28/29 July 1937 Fletcher experienced two seances at the Zimbabwe Temple with his 'guides'. They were absorbed for nine hours on each occasion with certain psychic communications relating to the origins of the ruins and the mysterious people who build the many edifices.

The great Phoenician sea journeys were described, and the Mediterranean connection of the former North African Nubian empires. Fletcher's guides quoted:

> Nubians they were called, who, owing to the various religious restrictions and persecutions … decided to set out to new lands. They were met by the companionship of those people who were called Hittites.

Joining forces they migrated and reached the ancient coast of Sofala, and their land journey commenced, encountering the fear of death from disease and fear of the unknown.

Fletcher again states:

> The whole country to Zimbabwe has a chain of similar fortresses, built by those ancient warriors. The evidence still exists of their perseverance, their integrity, their great religious principles, and their striving for freedom. On their journeys gold was worked from the bowels of the earth.

His guides continued. 2000 BC is what the guides said was the date of Zimbabwe's construction '... and that it took a hundred years to complete the building of the temple and the other buildings on the Acropolis'.

During those psychic episodes, some crucial information is revealed which points us again to remote civilisations and the worship those people practised.

The sacrificial altar points clearly to phallic worship, and the great similarities with the ruins of the Nauraghe type in Sardinia.

> Abbakuk the High Priest had been to perform the act of human sacrifice, but instead of him performing the rite upon someone else, he was stabbed to death by one of his victims. It was weird, it was strange: mere words cannot describe all that actually happened

writes Fletcher.

Anyone who is remotely familiar with psychic science will find Fletcher's breathtaking account of events at Zimbabwe highly entertaining, but it merely serves to add another piece to the puzzle.

About the inhabitants, Fletcher's guide transmits:

> The feasts lasted almost for a week until ill, overcome with gorging and various indulgences, they once more returned to a semblance of their normal condition in life.

Evidence of further ancient connections is given:

> On the western side of the Acropolis there are caves built which contained the regalia, the various dresses that had been worn by the priests of the early years.

This was the account of Ulali the last Queen, *c.* 500 BC, when the decline took place that led to the virtual extinction of the population remaining at Zimbabwe at the time.

Again Fletcher's psychic transmission gives us detailed accounts of events that took place:

> Fever again afflicted my people ... bodies withered and dropped by the wayside. There were no physicians, no men of healing, the salves which were so essential for the purposes of healing, were no longer obtainable ... . The valley was one of desolation.

It is worth noting that when Clarkson Fletcher experienced these psychic episodes he had indeed attended a lecture in Bulawayo in 1905 by Professor Randall-MacIver, an archaeologist who spent a few weeks at the ruins, as previously mentioned. Randall-MacIver insisted that the ruins could not be older than the fourteenth century. This of course was later disproved when the wood from the wall was carbon-dated to around AD 700.

Nevertheless, Fletcher's psychic experience with his guides may leave plenty of room for a mystical romanticised story of these ruins. He claims genuine experiences that were transmitted to him should be looked at with an understanding of psychic science and spiritual philosophy.

One of his guides, named as 'Lone Star', manifested and explained about the High Priest called Abbakuk who controlled the population of the Acropolis. The strictest laws were in existence. Those who offended the moral principles as set down by the High Priest suffered with their lives.

Their lives were instantly forfeited. Those who broke the rules and regulations drawn up for the safety of the inhabitants found no reprieve, no excuse. There was no avoidance of the penalty. Death and destruction came to them as the penalty for disobedience to the God of their lives. Sometimes the people had to fight in order to preserve their freedom, but it is fairly certain that no one ever came within five miles of those ruins, now so famous.

The information was given, says Fletcher, that writing was almost unknown in those days. There have been no documents, no weird carvings, no hieroglyphics found, making it difficult to trace the history of that civilisation which has now gone.

Whatever one thinks of these transmissions, they serve merely as an additional piece of a jigsaw puzzle about the builders of Zimbabwe.

There is only one direction where these people could have originated. If the events took place, then the ancient Phoenicians or Nubians were clearly the most likely peoples to have established a civilisation along the south-east African coast, as mentioned in Mutwa's tale.

For many centuries after the birth of Christ, these magnificent buildings slowly crumbled and disintegrated and were used by subsequent Bantu settlers. They were known to Arab merchants who, in their greed to find gold, took charge of the coastal waters and the ancient port of Sofala.

Communicating with the dead in these psychic sessions, Fletcher essentially presents a different viewpoint on Zimbabwe, its former inhabitants, and the importance of the rituals observed at that time.

V

A PUZZLE IN HEAVEN

Man fears time. But time fears the Sphinx.

Arab proverb

The civilisations of the Andes and Mexico, and in particular that elusive culture of the Mexican Olmecs, have many parallels between the 'First Time', or 'Zep Tepi' as it is known in Egyptian ancient history, and what we see in Zimbabwe.

The so-called anomaly of the location of the Giza pyramids themselves has only in recent years been explained in *The Orion Mystery*; an exact replica of the Orion belt being created by the complex of the pyramids on Earth, with the Nile drawing the Milky Way.

This 'celestial' phenomenon was not understood by Egyptologists simply because, as so often, scientists are narrowly studying what is their immediate interest (e.g. digging into the ground) instead of looking at the wider picture – in this case into the sky.

All ancient civilisations had a peculiar interest in star observation. That our forefathers had an understanding of astronomy way beyond what we have been able to grasp in our computer age is still not fully appreciated. For example, the passing on from generation to generation of the precise measurements of the Earth and the movements of the stars without the help of a computer suggests that, whoever these high civilisations were, they left us many unanswered questions.

The mystery of the many ruins left behind today in Zimbabwe, although some have been damaged over the centuries by treasure hunters and excavations, originates in a combination of events that took place in the distant past.

Whoever the original builders were, they had a purpose in mind which can only be connected to the times of the Phoenicians and their tremendous trading power as a seafaring nation.

The discovery of many gold-smelting sites in the vicinity of the various ruins suggests a civilisation that traded with Semitic races from at least 1500 BC, and the finding of Chinese pottery points to trading links with Asia.

Over many days and nights I gazed at the map of Africa and that of the world. The claim that Zimbabwe was built *circa* AD 500–700, from the carbon-dating of the wood found in one of the walls, somehow just did not add up.

It is known that over the centuries various settlements were based on the site, without giving proof as to the originators of the various buildings. Again I was drawn back to the ancient civilisations of Central America and of Egypt.

At first I could not believe my eyes. Had a I overlooked something so simple, yet so profoundly important? Could it be that the explanation of Zimbabwe and its connection with the 'First Time' in ancient civilisations lies in its cosmic mathematical location? There must be something that made the builders locate this settlement in the hills of Zimbabwe, not far from the shore of the Indian Ocean.

Gold? Fertile lands? There are plenty of lands along the East African shores that could have served as a location. But why here?

Here we must remind ourselves of what Plato, the great Greek writer, said about the ancient Egyptians:

> We Greeks are in reality children compared with this people with traditions ten times older, and as nothing of precious remembrance of the past would long survive in our country, Egypt has recorded and kept eternally the wisdom of the old times.

Unlocking the mystery

The location of the Pyramids of Giza, so clearly linked to the earliest time of mankind's high civilisation, is measured on the earth's map at longitude 31° 09′ east and latitude 29° 59′ north.

When we follow the line very slowly down from Giza right through the African continent, we arrive at longitude 31° 10′ 10″ east; a point exactly where the Great Zimbabwe ruins are located – virtually the same within a degree. This is precisely what the builders of Zimbabwe had in mind.

It seems that they so easily could have built nearer the coast, but specifically chose this location to align precisely with the concept of the earth and universe, as did the Egyptian pyramid builders. Every building had its function for the observation of the solar system, and that of specific dates in the calendar which were especially important to those cultures in their worshipping of the stars.

Let us recall the quote in Bent's *Ruined Cities of Mashonaland* from the work Swan contributed to the 'orientation and measurement of the Zimbabwe ruins'. He ends by saying: 'There are many astronomical points in these buildings to be yet considered.'

The labyrinthine nature of these buildings baffles description, yet Bent's evidence supporting the idea that the original buildings were erected by the 'Sea People' or

Phoenicians who practised the nature worship of Phoenicia was so often disputed.

The fact that the Giza pyramids of Egypt and the Zimbabwe ruins are built on virtually the same longitude cannot be a coincidence. The discoveries of the famous Zimbabwe bird representing Astarte, the female element in creation, and of the rosettes on stones, known as Phoenician emblems of the sun, are just two of many indicators. What we see is a deliberate building of a sky observatory at a dry location precisely aligned with the ancient Egyptian pyramids at Giza.

But of all the strange co-incidences we have seen in our journey to discover the builders of the heavenly ruins of Zimbabwe, one stands out: the fact that it was built by a people who had a clear understanding of astronomy, architecture and trade – people who understood the power of the stars and their influence on the Earth's position within the universe. It was a people who possessed the knowledge of the stars which was then so vital, especially for seafarers, navigating as the Phoenicians did across the great oceans mapping the world and trading with all continents of the earth.

The ancient civilisations of Egypt and South America had a number of sciences in common, such as star observation, architecture, numbers and the measurement of time.

A fine thread begins to stretch out in front of us on the face of the earth.

The Mexican connection

It is believed that about 20,000 BC people from Asia crossed a land bridge (where the Bering Strait now is) into North America and gradually migrated into what is now called Meso-America.

The countries of today, such as Mexico, Guatemala, Honduras, Belize and El Salvador, house a very large number of ancient cities and temples of the former Mayan civilisations. More specifically of interest are the many sites along the Yucatan and around the Gulf of Mexico: the Olmec cultures and the Mayan ruins of southern Mexico spring to mind. Around 2500 BC they established buildings and temples, and subsequent Maya civilisations developed their astronomical studies further.

It is beyond the scope of this book to explore the magnificent buildings and civilisations of central America, but the Mayas' obsession with observing the stars is of great interest in the context of Zimbabwe. Around the birth of Christ the Mayas had not only mastered mathematics but also perfected the most complex system of writing glyphs and, more importantly, created astrological calendars so immensely accurate that they could pinpoint any day within 370,000 years!

The Olmec culture of Mexico similarly continues to be a mystery. Here, unlike Zimbabwe's edifices, only large stone heads remain, but sculptured to a high degree, showing that around 1000 BC the Olmecs were advanced in certain sciences.

It is unfortunate that when the Spanish conquistadores arrived during the fifteenth century they brought with them not only gold-lusting explorers but also fanatical priests who ordered all Mayan literature to be burnt. Thus was destroyed one of the greatest heritages of knowledge on earth. The burning was so ruthless that only four of their sacred bark-paper books are preserved today – a cultural genocide that now leaves an immense gap in understanding the great advances the Mayas made in science. It is also believed, as with the great fire that destroyed the library of Alexandria in Egypt, that this Mayan literature housed the ancient records of mankind.

What we are left with around the world are great buildings, temples and irrigation systems that point to a civilisation well-versed in the sciences.

An exhaustive study of the connections that seem to exist at specific locations all over the globe is available to the reader from highly respected authors mentioned in the bibliography at the end of this book. More to the point, in Great Zimbabwe the remains of artefacts, sculptures and stone masonry carefully constructed to a high standard suggest links with other ancient civilisations.

That the Phoenicians were indeed in no small part responsible for the ongoing preservation of navigation, such as we have seen in their journeys around Africa long before Christ, is undoubtedly part of Zimbabwe's origins.

We must remind ourselves of the existence of such evidence as the Piri Reis map, which dates from around AD 1513 and was compiled by a Turkish seafarer who stated that it had been compiled from earlier sources dating back to Alexander the Great, who was born in 356 BC.

What this suggests is that sophisticated seafarers such as the Phoenicians did possess global maps dating far back into ancient times, despite the fact that historians keep telling us that their journeys were limited to their own shores.

The calendar

The seasonal changes were clearly observed in Zimbabwe, and even certain stars – quite consistent with previous ancient cultures around the world using their buildings as observatories and ceremonial locations. Also time itself was important to the ancients to convey a message. But what message? Writing would not, and mostly has not, survived on ancient buildings, but stars align with the earth at specific epochs, moving slowly and precisely. The originators of Zimbabwe would have been aware of the destruction of scripts, but the alignment of the buildings in conjunction with star constellations could pass a message far into the future.

Time units return with the precision of the day's sunrise and sunset – every day is like another day. Suddenly we find ourselves in a world that can be measured in absolute rather than relative terms (Bickermann's 'chronography').

This of course is quite different from Bickermann's 'calendariography', which in plain language deals with standard time measurement, i.e. what the ancients such as the Babylonians, Egyptians, Romans and Greeks developed, each in their own world and taking over their predecessors' knowledge.

The thirst for measuring time did not come from nowhere. Today's Gregorian calendar, in use almost everywhere, took a very long time indeed to be accepted widely.

Our Gregorian calendar is in effect the Roman calendar, which Julius Caesar reformed by establishing a year of 365 days with an added day, now 29 February, every four years to account for the difference between the solar and the common civil year.

When we gaze at the vastness of the night sky – the stars, the planets and the moon – the human eye observes these objects as if they were all the same distance. Of course thousands of such objects are scattered at varying distances in the universe.

During the course of the night, stars appear to rise in the east and set in the west: an apparent motion produced by the rotation of the earth. The apparent movement of the sun during the course of the day is better known.

The ancients started the tradition of dividing the night sky into constellations thousands of years ago, by assigning the names of their gods, heroes and fabled animals to certain star patterns.

It may seem obvious to us that the earth takes 365¼ days to orbit the sun. But the position of the sun can of course only directly be observed during a total solar eclipse, when brighter stars become visible.

The apparent path of the sun is known by astronomers as the ecliptic. For us it is mainly important to visualise the belt that surrounds the earth, which extends to the twelve constellations of the zodiac: Aries, Taurus, Gemini, Cancer, Leo, Virgo, Libra, Scorpius, Sagittarius, Capricorn, Aquarius and Pisces. The reader will be familiar with these star signs.

The earth slowly spins (clockwise from the viewpoint of the northern hemisphere) on its axis from east to west and thus moves in opposition to the direction of the planets' annual path around the sun.

At present the sun rises at vernal equinox due east between Pisces and Aquarius. Due to the effect of the axial precession of the earth, a very slight shift takes place through all twelve zodiac signs. Thus the sun spends 2160 years in each sign, completing a full circuit in 25,920 years. To sum up, the 'dawn' of Aquarius has arrived, with the vernal sun soon moving out of the age of Pisces.

The changes that took place were of immense importance to ancient cultures. With few exceptions, the proper motions of the stars are very small and almost undetectable over a human lifetime except with precise instruments.

When were the ancients really finding out about precession, which means that the earth's tilted axis lies broadside on to the sun twice a year? (This is when the equinoxes occur.) It is supposed to be a mystery but, according to the world's dictionaries, it was Hipparchus the great Greek astronomer who discovered the precession of the equinoxes. This notable discovery was the result of painstaking observations, worked upon by an acute mind.

Thousands of years before Christ, ancient cultures did indeed record just such astronomical events as the equinoxes. The Babylonians, for example, carried tokens in clay for accounting purposes.

The transition to written records of astronomical events came with the Sumerians. The written language emerged partly in their pictographs around 3000 BC: these cuneiform tablets revealed the first records of astronomical events, including the Sumerians' counting system based on the number 60.

This important number is clearly the key to Hipparchus' claim to fame for proposing precession as the explanation for the size of the annual change. He gave a value of 45′ or 46′ (seconds of arc), close to the figure of 50.274′ accepted today. This represents a distance of just under one-sixtieth of one degree, so that it takes 72 years for the sun to migrate just one degree along the ecliptic. 72 years is an entire lifetime, considering that in Hipparchus' time around 120 BC the average lifespan was no more than 40 years.

Hipparchus' discovery must be questioned: what is claimed as a discovery might well be a rediscovery from ancient cultures such as the Sumerians, and I dare say possibly they acquired this knowledge from a more remote civilisation.

Just as with the ancient Egyptians and ancient Mayas, the rituals that took place at the Zimbabwe buildings point to the observation of certain stars and changes in seasons.

It also happens that the age of Pisces is at an end and we are moving into the next zodiac sign of Aquarius – a time of great change which the Mexican Mayas and the Egyptians were acutely aware of.

Some vital astronomical events took place that would have been observed at Zimbabwe, as we have seen in previous chapters, marking the beginning of each of the four seasons. All ancient cultures celebrated these moments such as the winter and summer solstices and the spring and autumn equinoxes.

As a point of reminder, in the northern hemisphere the winter solstice falls on 21 December and the summer solstice, the longest day, on 21 June.

In the southern hemisphere of the globe these dates are reversed, with winter beginning on 21 June and summer on 21 December. This applies to the location of the Zimbabwe Ruins.

Ancient World Wide Web

> The reed-floats of the sky are set in place for me, that
> I may cross by means of them to Re at the horizon ...
> I will stand among them, for the moon is my brother,
> the Morning Star is my offspring ...
>
> *The New Osiris in the Pyramid Texts (c. 2400 BC)*

The new millennium in our Western calendar has become a milestone thanks to the discovery of many ancient sites around the world where we can at last begin to make sense of the signs that have been with mankind for thousands of years. Atlantis, the Mu Empire and other mythologies stretching back to 8000 BC and beyond should not be discounted.

Take the Mesopotamian flood story as recorded by the Sumerians on tablets dating around 3000 BC. Stories were handed down through the generations, and the tablets show that even then the story had been around for a long time. No scholar has yet been able to date the creation of such myths – we simply do not know how long this 'baggage' of myths has been around mankind.

A very detailed study of how mythologies carry legends of the 'First Time' in history, from which no written records have survived, is indeed available in Hertha von Dechend's and George Santillana's *Hamlet's Mill*.

They stated that human knowledge was certainly transmitted via the mythologies, so similar around the globe; most importantly the repeat of a major catastrophe such as the flood and the darkening of the skies far back in time.

Recent research has shown that the Egyptian pyramids and the Sphinx may date back to a much more remote time than previously assumed – possibly between 10500 and 8000 BC.

As the mist rises over the hills of the Zimbabwe Ruins in the early morning sun, as it has done since the 'First Time', it becomes apparent that these buildings were clearly designed to function within a culture that understood the importance of the various sciences that are required to progress to such a high standard of building.

It is now time to recapture the location of Zimbabwe on the earth's map. It is located at longitude 31° 10′ 10″ east and latitude 20° 16′ 30″ south. At this junction Zimbabwe lies on the 'navel' with the Giza plateau in Egypt.

We can imagine the high priests of this civilisation observing the stars – most remarkably, only northern ones, as the position of the altar and the centre of the small temple at the Enclosure point to true north when one draws a straight line passing through the outer wall where the gap is placed.

It is then possible to observe 680 yards away in the distance, continuing in the straight line of the meridian, a great imposing rock on the hill, also called the Acropolis. The straight line is certainly no coincidence. We could interpret this as a double observation of the same meridian transit.

Swan tells us more:

> ... The parallel lines would imply that stars did not pass over the stone but disappeared and reappeared behind it. Looking from the altar it would disappear and at the same instant reappear to an observer at [particular] points ...

Swan further points out that, as the apparent height of the middle of the stone as seen from the centre of the arcs is 7½° and the latitude of Zimbabwe is 20° 16′ 30″, we are looking at stars with a north polar distance of around 28°.

Curiously he then states that the star that may have been observed on those two lines 'admits of calculation', implying that the people who built Zimbabwe and made observations there go too far back in time: indeed a most peculiar statement.

Again the number game seems to give an ancient connection between Zimbabwe and Giza. For example, there are 28 steps in the Grand Gallery that leads up to the King's Chamber in the Great Pyramid. In addition the Sphinx Temple had 28 pillars. More remarkable is the discovery by Rand Flem-Ath that the Sphinx Temple had a 28° bearing from the mortuary temple of the Great Pyramid, and that if this bearing is extended it points literally like a marker to what he calls the Hudson Bay Pole.

Because of the right ascension that all stars undergo in a very slow but regular movement, it would be a wild guess to pin down a specific star that would have hit the meridian line on the night of a major festivity in ancient times.

I was still searching for reasons for the location and star observation in Zimbabwe at a time which could fit with the features that are so striking, such as the patterns on the outer wall, clearly pointing to the solstices.

In our modern times, remarkably accurate computer software for sky charting is capable of giving us a view of the sky far back in time.

★★★

> The gods who are in the sky are brought to you, the gods who are on earth assemble for you …
>
> *Pyramid Texts*

The ancient Egyptians' obsession with star observation took various forms. Most strikingly the stars were thought to describe the journey of a Pharaoh's life and his afterlife, or preparation for the underworld, ascending to the sky or stairway of heaven.

It is therefore not surprising that Orion and Ra, the sun, are of immense importance in that mythology. With the approach of night the strength of Ra, the sun god of Heliopolis, got weaker. The solar boat entered the realm of night and met the powers of darkness. The chief of these was the serpent Apep, who tried to swallow the boat. Then a nightly struggle ensued. When the sun reappeared on the eastern horizon the next day, prayers of thankfulness were offered that Ra was triumphant and that the sun, source of warmth and light, would continue to shine.

That the Phoenicians had similar beliefs of sun worship we saw from the various symbols they used, as mentioned in earlier chapters.

A similar procession of preparation to the underworld and star worshipping must have been part of the original plans of the builders of Zimbabwe, but why did they go to such lengths to align the buildings?

A good description comes from the Pyramid Texts, which show the ascent of the departed king to the sky. He joins Orion (Osiris) and Sirius is his guide. Both continue together as participants in the cosmic cycle. The spirits of the dead hope to join the never-setting, never-dying, circumpolar stars.

These two possible transfigurations, in which the dead pharaoh joins Osiris or the circumpolar stars, may explain the orientation of the so-called air shafts from the King's Chamber in the Great Pyramid: the shafts may be ramps by which the dead king makes his way to heaven.

In Bauval's *The Orion Belt*, the Egyptian engineer proves in detail how the Great Pyramid's air shafts were precisely aligned with constellations in the sky at certain epochs. Most important was Orion, being the most prominent stellar alignment mirroring Giza in around 10,500 BC.

Can we find a similar scenario in Zimbabwe? In fact the sky chart computer simulations can make this an exciting proposition. When looking at the night sky in 500 BC we will find our first clue to what the ancient priests of Zimbabwe observed.

The buildings point to the northern hemisphere observation of the sky, despite the fact that the people lived in the southern hemisphere. It is possible to assume that these stargazers originated from the northern hemisphere.

The reader will recall the altars and gaps in the wall in the Enclosure pointing in a straight line true north towards the hill complex.

At midnight of the summer solstice (in December in the southern hemisphere) we would have observed true north – hovering brightly above us is the great figure of Orion. At first this is significant enough, but at a closer look we find that the brightest of all three stars in Orion's belt, Al Nitak (Zeta Orionis), sits directly true north towards the polar.

Orion is identified by the ancient Egyptians with Osiris, their high god of resurrection and rebirth but also the legendary bringer of civilisation to the Nile Valley in the

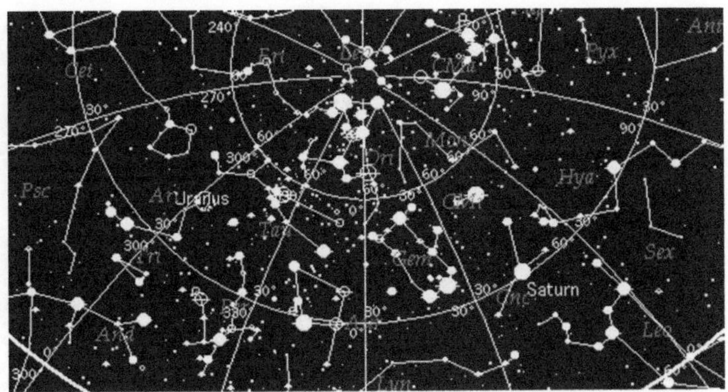

The sky looking north from Zimbabwe, 500 BC

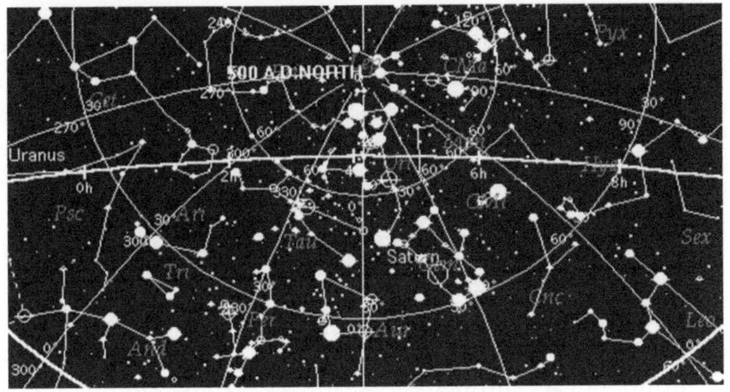

The sky looking north from Zimbabwe, 500 AD

remote epoch known to the ancient Egyptians as the 'First Time' or 'Zep Tepi'.

Now, this observation is significant because, when we look at AD 500, one thousand years later, which is the time when archaeologists think Zimbabwe was first settled, Orion would have shifted off the true north alignment. When looking even at around 700 AD, no major stars are aligned true north at the summer solstice.

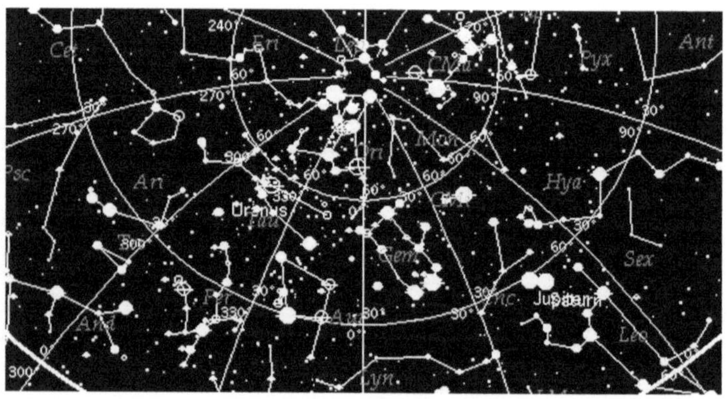

The sky looking north from Zimbabwe, 1000 BC

The quest to find a time of importance to the stargazers of Zimbabwe is thus moving to a date of 500 BC, and not only because of the true north alignment of Al Nitak. There is also the most remarkable mirror image of the ruins of Matindela's circular foundations and of Orion (also known as the hunter or warrior) holding his club raised on a straight line with Al Nitak and defending himself with his shield.

This shield of stars, out of which four are sparkling bright in the night sky of 500 BC, would have given the builders of Zimbabwe a mirror of Matindela. These circular foundations are directed west, as is the shield of Orion in the sky when looking true north from the ruins in 500 BC.

When we now examine the sky chart projected into the more distant past, a very interesting view becomes visible. Orion and his defensive shield look at us on the summer solstice (that is, 21 December) in 4000 BC, having moved well off the pole position. But in 1500 BC Orion is again correctly aligned north, with its bottom star Saiph pointing directly north.

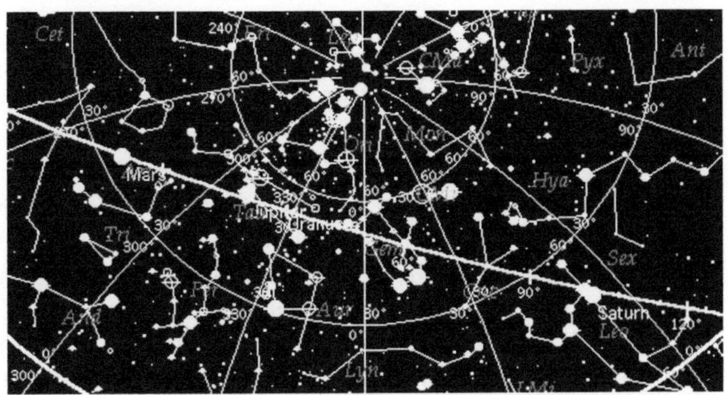

The sky looking north from Zimbabwe, 1500 BC

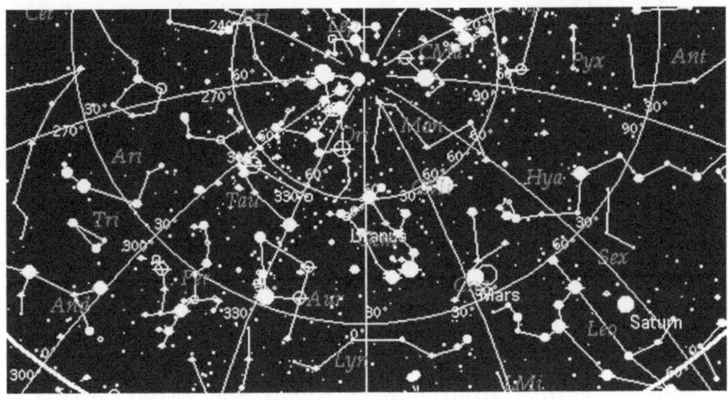

The sky looking north from Zimbabwe, 2000 BC

We know that the height of the Phoenicians' power was the period from around 1000 to 500 BC: in fact Phoenicia had declined by 300 BC.

The reader will recall that the Phoenicians are known to have circumnavigated Africa as early as 600 BC, and thus could have been the original builders of Zimbabwe.

Is this not a connection that leads to ancient civilisations communicating in similar ways through architecture, astronomy and geometry? Their gods may have different names, but their symbols are so similar across the world that a one-time source of all this knowledge surely must have existed.

The phallic symbols, such as the great conical tower in the Enclosure, are one of many examples. The Zimbabwe birds that were found are another example. Again here is the mystery of the bird that is so similar to the Egyptian god-king Horus, depicted so often as a falcon or hawk. To appreciate the importance and meaning of the birds prominently found at Zimbabwe, the Egyptian beliefs give us a good pointer.

Horus is regarded as the 'dweller on the horizon', for which the Egyptians built temples in his honour. Interestingly, Horakhti or 'Horus of the Horizon' was often shown in Egyptian reliefs as a man with a hawk's head, on top of which rests the solar disc. At the temple of Edfu in Egypt is a prominent stone statue of a falcon quite similar to those that were found at Zimbabwe.

This points possibly to an ancient reminder of beliefs dating back to the Egyptians and the importance they placed on the skies.

The Pharaohs of Egypt were indeed of the line of Horus, and through that they all descended directly from the heavenly father Osiris. Their star observations only made sense precisely because of this all-important relationship with the myth of Osiris.

The mythology of Osiris, and his misfortune of not reproducing with his wife Isis, gave rise to the myth of the boy Horus being conceived *after Osiris himself had died*. This child was deified and called Horus, and we know him to be the important sun god. As I have previously mentioned, Horus was depicted in many forms such as a falcon's head. It is said that one eye of the falcon represents the sun and the other the moon.

Astronomically this suggests that the ancient Egyptians did notice the sun and the moon as the same size, as indeed they appear when looking from the Earth.

Here we find a striking similarity on the carved birds found at Zimbabwe – two clearly marked circles on either side and to the front of the statue.

The Zimbabwe birds are about 355 mm high and a few surmount columns that are up to 914 mm high. They are not carved of wood but from a soft green-grey soapstone talc that is fairly common in central and northern Zimbabwe.

Global connect

Theories have been around for some time that Zimbabwe could have flourished by itself without outside civilisations, but I could not disagree more. The sky charts have given us a most direct reminder of the precise star alignments that were visible during the night at Zimbabwe, when the high priests would have observed the heavens.

Our question about the location of Zimbabwe – in this remote spot, but aligned with the Giza pyramids – could surely be answered with a much deeper question: where to look?

With the world map spread out on the floor, my eyes gazed over the major ancient sites currently known to us from explorations around the world.

The way we look at maps today is of course by assuming that Greenwich is the navel of the globe. For a moment I ignored this relatively recent way of organising the world. Instead I concentrated on Giza, without doubt the most sacred site in the world known to mankind at present.

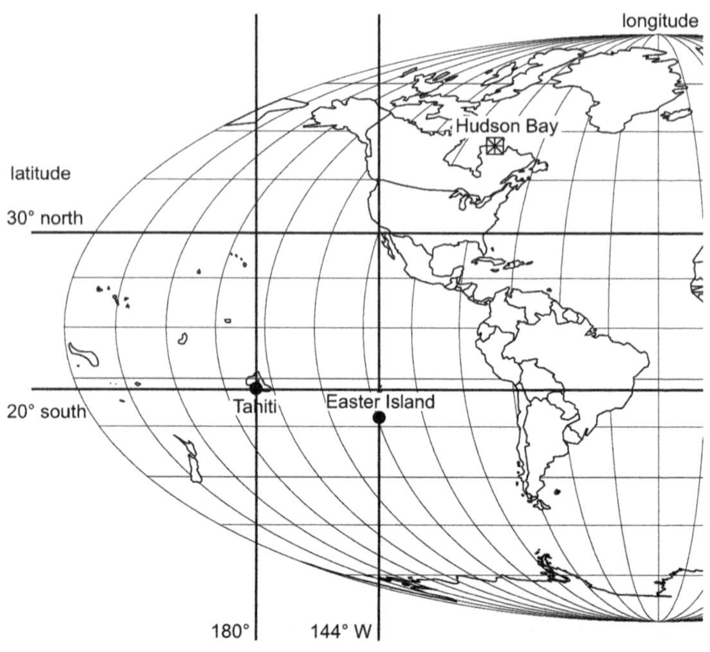

Major ancient sites across the globe

Slowly follow a line from the Giza plateau in Egypt down through the African continent until it hits Zimbabwe virtually on the same longitude at 31° east. This could be by chance, but when we look across the world to other ancient buildings we will find a most extraordinary connection.

Our own navel of the world is set at Greenwich as zero degrees, but why?

In October 1884 representatives of twenty-five European countries gathered in Washington DC to make a final decision as to where to locate the prime meridian of the world. Over the centuries the various European powers disagreed and built their own observatories, usually in their respective capitals. By 1884 it finally became apparent

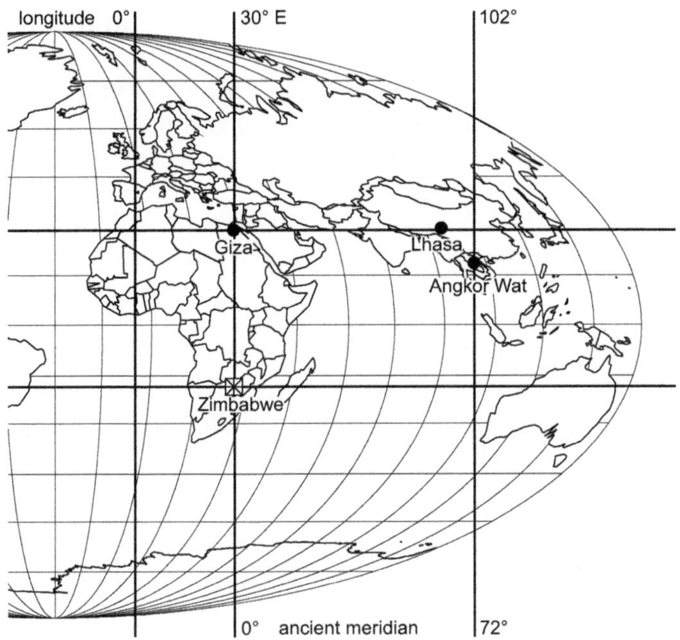

that one universal meridian needed to be set. Greenwich was a favourite candidate purely because of the Port of London's busy shipping. So it was agreed to set the prime meridian at Greenwich. This was despite the fact that the then Astronomer Royal for Scotland, Professor Charles Smyth, argued that the Great Pyramid of Egypt would be the ideal choice as the prime meridian, mainly because the meridian line would then pass over the maximum possible amount of land. It would also acknowledge the Pyramid as the grandest monument on the globe.

It was not to be.

Let us focus our attention on the world map in front of us for a moment.

Moving slowly eastward along the globe from Greenwich at 0° we eventually hit 30° east, the longitude where Giza and the ancient Pyramids are located. On this ancient longitude we find Zimbabwe placed at latitude 20° south – and, to be precise, on longitude 31° east, a variation of 1° from Giza.

One of the key numbers we are dealing with here is 72: it in fact relates to the key planetary mechanisms of the earth. This is the fixed and apparently eternal precession of the earth's axis of rotation around the pole of the ecliptic, a point at which the sun appears at the equinoxes and the solstices around the sky at the rate of one degree every 72 years. This figure also amounts to 30°, or one complete zodiacal constellation, every 2160 years.

If we then go back to the globe and add 72° from Giza, we end up at 102.5° east at Angkor Wat, the great ancient city located in Cambodia.

Let us just suppose we look at the world differently for a moment.

Instead of using Greenwich as a starting point, to map the world the ancients would have used as a navel or centre Giza in Egypt at 0°. If we do so, going east across the globe we find Angkor Wat at around 72° east. If it is a coincidence that the location of Zimbabwe is on the same longitude as the Pyramids, then we must look further.

Doubling 72° makes 144°, and following eastwards on the map from Angkor Wat we find ourselves in the middle of the Pacific Ocean. Sure enough, there is near this 144° degree line a very ancient monument called Easter Island. The island is one of many mysteries in the world, with its great statues overlooking the Pacific Ocean but aiming towards the skies.

This ancient mapping of the world through star observation points to a few other significant megalithic structures in the Pacific.

When drawing a line 108° east of Angkor Wat, we will hit a point in Tahiti which is also located near enough latitude 20° south, exactly where Zimbabwe is located. Going east from Giza, this would lead to precisely 180° at the point of Tahiti, as if this was to be the ancient date line.

Looking at this astonishing new or ancient mapping of the world with various observatories (if you like) spread across the world, then in that context Zimbabwe would have been an important part of the ancient network.

The fact that major stars were precisely aligned at Zimbabwe in 500 BC gives us a mirror of what the people who build these structures saw in the skies at that time. The great enclosure of Zimbabwe marks an observatory built by ancient people whose origin could lie in north Africa, as all their observations, it seems, were directed towards the northern heavens.

In the context of the builders of Zimbabwe and the geometric coincidence of its location, virtually on the same longitude as the Giza pyramids of Egypt, we can only ask: was it a random location, or planned?

The conical tower at Zimbabwe points clearly to a very remote time, a time of Phoenician and Egyptian influence; a time when its builders were occupied not only with the nature of phallic ceremonies but more visually with the study of the heavens.

From earliest times man was preoccupied with observing the stars. This took on different forms.

In 1999 the European Southern Observatory was established in northern Chile, in the barren landscape of the Atacama desert over 8000 feet above sea level, far from civilisation. One of the world's most powerful observatories has been erected here to accommodate four gigantic telescopes, each 27 feet in diameter. Guided by the most advanced computers, 430 tons of glass and steel focus on the heavens. It is here that astronomers have access to the largest telescope system on earth and to unveil further mysteries of the universe.

The ancients would possibly have envied this technology, but going back over 2000 years we find that very detailed knowledge existed concerning the earth and other planets. Zimbabwe was part of an ancient universe observation net that connected the globe and seems to extend far back, even beyond the earliest Egyptian records of star observation.

We now know the likely epoch of the builders and the significant location of Zimbabwe in a world-wide map, but Giza is indeed not the most ancient meridian line.

Archaeological and geological radiocarbon dates have proved unequivocally that the last catastrophe on earth occurred around 9600 BC.

The scholar Charles Hapgood showed in *The Path of the Pole*, based on geological evidence, that the arctic magnetic pole shifted from its previous location at Hudson Bay to the location that we know today.

The last crustal movement on earth began, says Flem-Ath, around 15,000 BC and lasted to about 10,000 BC.

The so-called Hudson Bay pole, located then at 60° N, 83° W is of great interest, as Flem-Ath showed by locating what he calls 'sacred latitudes'. If in remote times, such as before 9600 BC, the pole was indeed positioned at Hudson Bay, then surely some very ancient sacred sites would be located on a sacred latitude pointing to Hudson Bay, he argues. And indeed his thought-provoking research points out some ground-breaking discoveries.

During the period of the Hudson Bay Pole, Giza was at 15″ north, and the Tibetan holy city of Lhasa at 0°, the Equator. Tahiti, which is the nearest land site in the Pacific, corresponds to the ancient web already mentioned when we focus on the Giza meridian, which in turn incorporates Zimbabwe as a sacred site.

Controversial material has been published over the past 100 years, some by archaeologists mentioned previously, who indeed did make great efforts to put the Great Zimbabwe ruins into the southern African context.

Times, though, have moved on.

That Zimbabwe is part of an ancient network beyond the shores of Africa has been shown by the map of the world.

It seems quite prevalent in the academic world to ignore any new controversial findings that might shed light on unresolved questions about significant historical events. Fortunately though, in recent decades new research methods and the pioneering work of many authors mentioned have shaken the foundations of schoolbook history that has been proved quite inaccurate in the dating of our ancient past. It should be of worldwide historical interest to put the record straight.

In *The Structure of Scientific Revolutions*, Kuhn argued that scientists are mistaken to think of the pursuit of science as a detached and unemotional activity. By becoming comfortable with a certain theory, they develop an emotional attachment. Once anyone challenges their theories, they become defensive.

The great new discoveries and scientific revolutions by Copernicus, Newton and Einstein encountered extreme resistance purely because of these established and entrenched opinions held by other scientists for a lifetime. Kuhn suggests that it takes an overwhelming proof to convince established scientists to change their thinking, once they are stuck with a theory.

Mutwa's tale of the southern African mythologies and the invasion of southern Africa by foreign people arriving in big ships in remote times should not be taken lightly. Oral history, passed on between the generations, has existed for many thousands of years all over the globe.

There remains little doubt that the pointers we receive from the charts that I have discussed and the global mapping of major ancient sites represent the accumulation of ancient knowledge. So far we have seen little evidence of instruments that these ancients could have used to make precise mappings of the world, except that we do know of maps of Antarctica that pre-date the voyages of Columbus. The fact that the Phoenicians made voyages across the oceans around 1000 BC with maps we have not yet seen suggests that an advanced civilisation must have existed at a remote time, with knowledge of the earth's measurements.

Hapgood comments:

> ... the trigonometry of the projection (in relation to the size of the Earth) suggests the work of Alexandrian geographers, but the evident knowledge of longitude implies a people unknown to us.

That Zimbabwe was part of an ancient observation network that stretches across the globe rings loud and clear in the true words of John Michell when he said:

> A great scientific instrument lies sprawled over the entire surface of the globe. At some period, perhaps 4,000 years ago, almost every corner of the world was visited by a group of men who came with a particular task to accomplish.

Great Zimbabwe's remains are the pointer to an ancient Giza connection, precisely aligned in that instrument to map the world.

An explanation of exactly what task these great seafarers and builders were trying to accomplish lies, I suspect, in the ancient history of even earlier civilisations that possessed advanced knowledge in astronomy, architecture, mathematics and related sciences.

Bibliography

Eric Axeldon, *Early Portuguese Explorers, Congo to Cape*, London, 1973

G. von Schubert, *Heinrich Barth, der Bahnbrecher der deutschen Afrikaforschung*, Berlin, Reimer, 1897

R. Bauval and A. Gilbert, *The Orion Mystery*, Heinemann, 1994

D.N. Beach, *The Shona and Zimbabwe, 900–1850*, London, 1980

J. Theodore Bent, *The Ruined Cities of Mashonaland*, London, Longmans, 1892

C.R. Boxer, *Four Centuries of Portuguese Expansion 1415–1825*, Johannesburg, Witwatersrand University Press, 1961

E.E. Burke (ed.), *The Journal of Carl Mauch, His Travels in the Transvaal and Rhodesia, 1869–1872*, Salisbury, National Archives of Rhodesia, 1969

A.J. Clement, *The Kalahari and its Lost City*, Cape Town, Longmans, 1967

Basil Davidson, *The Lost Cities of Africa*, Boston, MA, Little, Brown & Co., 1959

Jose Maria D'Eca De Queiroz, *Seara Dos Tempos*, Lisbon, 1969

C. Ehret, 'Patterns of Bantu and Central Sudanic settlement in central and southern Africa (1000 BC–500 AD)', *Journal of Transafrican History*, University of California, 1973, vol. 3, pp.1-71

Rand and Rose Flem-Ath, *When the Sky Fell: In Search of Atlantis*, Toronto, Stoddart, 1995 (Website: www.flem-ath.com)

H.C. Fletcher, *Psychic Episodes of Great Zimbabwe*, Bulawayo, 1939

P. Garlake, *Life at Great Zimbabwe*, Harare, Mambo Press, 1982

R. Gayre, *Origin of the Zimbabwean Civilisation*, Harare, Galaxie, 1973

Ignaz Goldzhier, *Mythology among the Hebrews and its Historical Development*, London, 1877

M. Guillain, *L'Afrique Orientale*, Documents

Rider Haggard, *King Solomon's Mines*, Oxford, 1989

M. Hall, *The Changing Past: Farmers, Kings and Traders in Southern Africa 200–1860 AD*, London, J Currey, 1987

R. Hall, *The Ancient Ruins of Rhodesia*, Methuen, 1902

——, *Great Zimbabwe*, Methuen, 1905

Graham Hancock, *Fingerprints of the Gods*, London, Mandarin, 1996

Charles H. Hapgood, *Earth's Shifting Crust: A key to some basic problems of earth science*, New York, Pantheon, 1958; revised and reissued as *The Path of the Pole*, Philadelphia, Chilton, 1970

——, *Maps of the Ancient Sea Kings: Evidence of advanced civilization in the ice age*, New York, Chilton, 1966

Gerhard Herm, *The Phoenicians*, New York, Morrow, 1975

O. Hope, *6000 Years of Seafaring*, self-published, Gastonia, NC, 1983

T.N. Huffman, *The Soapstone Birds from Great Zimbabwe*, African Arts, 1985

—— and J.C. Vogel, *The Chronology of Great Zimbabwe*, unpublished, 1986

W. Keller, *The Bible as History*, New York, Morrow, 1956

Johannes Kepler, *New Astronomy*, Cambridge Press, 1989

Thomas S. Kuhn, *The Structure of Scientific Revolutions*, University of Chicago Press, 1970

F. Lenormant, in *Revue de l'Histoire des Religions*, Paris, 1881

J.D. Lewis-Williams, *Believing and Seeing: Symbolic meanings in southern San rock paintings*, London, Academic Press, 1981

Graham Lord, *Ghosts of King Solomon's Mines, Mozambique and Zimbabwe: A quest*, London, Sinclair Stevenson, 1991

Wilfrid Mallows, *Mystery of the Great Zimbabwe: A new solution*, New York, Norton, 1984

K.N. Mufuka, *Dzimbahwe: Life and politics in the golden age (1100–1500 AD)*, Harare Publishing House, 1983

Otto Neugebauer, *History of Ancient Mathematical Astronomy*, Springer, 1975

B. Paver, *Zimbabwe Cavalcade*, London, Cassell, 1957

G. Perrot and C. Chipiez, *Histoire de l'Art dans l'Antiquité*, Paris, Hachette, 1882

H. Philby, *The Queen of Sheba*, London, Quartet, 1981

Ptolemy, *The Almagest*, tr. G.J. Toomer, London, Duckworth, 1984

D. Randall-McIver, *Mediaeval Rhodesia*, London, Macmillan, 1906

R. Kent Rasmussen, *Historical Dictionary of Rhodesia/Zimbabwe*, Metuchen, NJ, Scarecrow Press, 1979

Giorgio de Santillana and Hertha von Dechend, *Hamlet's Mill: An essay investigating the origins of human knowledge and its transmission through myth*, Boston, Nonpareil Books, 1977

Robert Schoch, *Voices of the Rocks: A scientist looks at catastrophes and ancient civilizations*, New York, Harmony Books, 1999

Somerby, *Bible Myths and their Parallels in Other Religions*, New York, 1882

R. Summers, 'The Dating of the Zimbabwe Ruins', *Antiquity*, 1955, vol. 29, pp.107–11

——, *Zimbabwe: A Rhodesian mystery*, Nelson, Johannesburg, 1963

Theil, *Das Phoenizische Alterthum*, Berlin

Gertrude Caton Thompson, *Zimbabwe Culture, Ruins and Reactions*, Oxford, Clarendon Press, 1931

Lawrence Vambe, *An Ill-fated People: Zimbabwe before and after Rhodes*, University of Pittsburgh, PA, 1973

I. Velikovsky, *Peoples of the Sea*, New York, Doubleday, 1977

J.A. West, *The Serpent in the Sky*, New York, Harper & Row, 1979

Phil Whitaker, *Eclipse of the Sun*, London, Phoenix House, 1997

H.A. Wieschhoff, *The Zimbabwe-Monomotapa Culture in South-east Africa*, Menasha, USA, George Banta, 1941

J. Gardner Wilkinson, *The Ancient Egyptians*, London, J. Murray, 1836

A. Wilmot, *Monomotapa (Rhodesia)*, London, 1896

Software

Skymap Pro Version 6, developed and marketed by Chris Marriott (chris@skymap.com)

SD - #0022 - 070726 - C0 - 197/132/6 - PB - 9781844261116 - Gloss Lamination